# WHAT DOES THE BIBLE *Really* TEACH?

## Large-Print Edition

# THIS BOOK IS THE PROPERTY OF

PUBLISHERS
Watchtower Bible and Tract Society of New York, Inc.
Brooklyn, New York, U.S.A.

Unless otherwise indicated, Scripture quotations
are from the modern-language
*New World Translation of the Holy Scriptures
—With References*

*What Does the Bible Really Teach?*
*—Large Print*
English (*bhlp*-E)

Made in the United States of America

# CONTENTS

# Is This What God Purposed?

READ any newspaper. Look at television, or listen to the radio. There are so many stories of crime, war, and terrorism! Think about your own troubles. Perhaps illness or the death of a loved one is causing you great distress. You may feel like the good man Job, who said that he was "drenched with misery."—Job 10:15, *The Holy Bible in the Language of Today.*

Ask yourself:

- Is this what God purposed for me and for the rest of mankind?
- Where can I find help to cope with my problems?
- Is there any hope that we will ever see peace on the earth?

The Bible provides satisfying answers to these questions.

## THE BIBLE TEACHES THAT
## GOD WILL BRING ABOUT
## THESE CHANGES ON THE EARTH

*"He will wipe out every tear
from their eyes, and death will be no more, neither
will mourning nor outcry nor pain be anymore."
—Revelation 21:4*

*"The lame one will climb up just as a stag does."
—Isaiah 35:6*

*"The eyes of the blind ones will be opened."
—Isaiah 35:5*

*"All those in the memorial tombs will . . . come out."
—John 5:28, 29*

*"No resident will say: 'I am sick.'"
—Isaiah 33:24*

*"There will come to be
plenty of grain on the earth."—Psalm 72:16*

# BENEFIT FROM WHAT THE BIBLE TEACHES

Do not quickly dismiss what is presented on the preceding pages as mere wishful thinking. God has promised to bring these things about, and the Bible explains how he will do so.

But the Bible does more than that. It provides the key to your enjoying a truly satisfying life even now. Think for a moment about your own anxieties and troubles. They may include money matters, family problems, loss of health, or the death of a loved one. The Bible can help you to deal with problems today, and it can provide relief by answering such questions as these:

- *Why do we suffer?*
- *How can we cope with life's anxieties?*
- *How can we make our family life happier?*
- *What happens to us when we die?*
- *Will we ever see our dead loved ones again?*
- *How can we be sure that God will fulfill his promises for the future?*

The fact that you are reading this book shows that you would like to find out what the Bible teaches. This book will help you. Notice that the paragraphs have corresponding questions at the bottom of the page.

*What Does the Bible Really Teach?*

Millions have enjoyed using the question-and-answer method when discussing the Bible with Jehovah's Witnesses. We hope you will too. May you have God's blessing as you now enjoy the thrilling and satisfying experience of learning what the Bible *really* teaches!

## GET TO KNOW YOUR BIBLE

THERE are 66 books and letters that make up the Bible. These are divided into chapters and verses for easy reference. When scriptures are cited in this publication, the first number after the name indicates the chapter of the Bible book or letter, and the next refers to the verse. For example, the citation "2 Timothy 3:16" means the second letter to Timothy, chapter 3, verse 16.

You will quickly become familiar with the Bible by looking up the scriptures cited in this publication. Also, why not start a program of daily Bible reading? By reading three to five chapters a day, you can read the entire Bible in a year.

# CHAPTER ONE

# What Is the Truth About God?

**Does God really care about you?**

**What is God like? Does he have a name?**

**Is it possible to get close to God?**

HAVE you ever noticed the way children ask questions? Many start asking as soon as they learn to speak. With wide, eager eyes, they look up at you and ask such things as: Why is the sky blue? What are the stars made of? Who taught the birds to sing? You may try hard to answer, but it is not always easy. Even your best answer may lead to yet another question: Why?

² Children are not the only ones who ask questions. As we grow up, we keep asking. We do this in order to find our way, to learn of dangers that we need to avoid, or to satisfy our curiosity. But many people seem to stop asking questions, especially the most important ones. At least, they stop searching for the answers.

1, 2. Why is it often good to ask questions?

³ Think about the question on the cover of this book, the questions raised in the preface, or those at the beginning of this chapter. These are some of the most important questions you can ask. Yet, many people have given up trying to find the answers. Why? Does the Bible have the answers? Some feel that its answers are too hard to understand. Others worry that asking questions could lead to shame or embarrassment. And some decide that such questions are best left to religious leaders and teachers. What about you?

⁴ Very likely you are interested in getting answers to life's big questions. No doubt you sometimes wonder: 'What is the purpose of life? Is this life all there is? What is God really like?' It is good to ask such questions, and it is important that you do not give up until you find satisfying, reliable answers. The famous teacher Jesus Christ said: "Keep on asking, and it will be given you; keep on seeking,

**3.** Why do many stop trying to find answers to the questions that matter most?

**4, 5.** What are some of the most important questions we can ask in life, and why should we seek the answers?

and you will find; keep on knocking, and it will be opened to you."—Matthew 7:7.

⁵ If you "keep on seeking" for answers to the important questions, you will find that the search can be very rewarding. (Proverbs 2:1-5) Despite what other people may have told you, there *are* answers, and you *can* find them—in the Bible. The answers are not too hard to understand. Better yet, they bring hope and joy. And they can help you to live a satisfying life right now. To begin, let us consider a question that has troubled many people.

## IS GOD UNCARING AND HARDHEARTED?

⁶ Many people think that the answer to that question is yes. 'If God cared,' they reason, 'would not the world be a very different place?' We look around and see a world full of war, hatred, and misery. And as individuals, we get sick, we suffer, we lose loved ones in death. Thus, many say, 'If God cared about us and our problems, would he not prevent such things from happening?'

6. Why do many people think that God is uncaring when it comes to human suffering?

*What Does the Bible Really Teach?*

⁷ Worse yet, religious teachers sometimes lead people to think that God is hardhearted. How so? When tragedy strikes, they say that it is God's will. In effect, such teachers blame God for the bad things that happen. Is that the truth about God? What does the Bible really teach? James 1:13 answers: "When under trial, let no one say: 'I am being tried by God.' For with evil things God cannot be tried nor does he himself try anyone." So God is *never* the source of the wickedness you see in the world around you. (Job 34:10-12) Granted, he does allow bad things to happen. But there is a big difference between *allowing* something to happen and *causing* it.

⁸ For example, think about a wise and loving father with a grown son who is still living at home with his parents. When the son becomes rebellious

---

7. (a) How have religious teachers led many to think that God is hardhearted? (b) What does the Bible really teach about the trials we may suffer?

8, 9. (a) How might you illustrate the difference between allowing wickedness to exist and causing it? (b) Why would it be unfair for us to find fault with God's decision to allow mankind to pursue a wayward course?

*What Is the Truth About God?*

and decides to leave home, his father does not stop him. The son pursues a bad way of life and gets into trouble. Is the father the *cause* of his son's problems? No. (Luke 15:11-13) Similarly, God has not stopped humans when they have chosen to pursue a bad course, but he is not the *cause* of the problems that have resulted. Surely, then, it would be unfair to blame God for all the troubles of mankind.

⁹ God has good reasons for allowing mankind to follow a bad course. As our wise and powerful Creator, he does not have to explain his reasons to us. Out of love, however, God does this. You will learn more about these reasons in Chapter 11. But rest assured that God is not responsible for the problems we face. On the contrary, he gives us the only hope for a solution!—Isaiah 33:2.

¹⁰ Furthermore, God is holy. (Isaiah 6:3) This means that he is pure and clean. There is no trace of badness in him. So we can trust him complete-

**10. Why can we trust that God will undo all the effects of wickedness?**

*What Does the Bible Really Teach?*

ly. That is more than we can say for humans, who sometimes become corrupt. Even the most honest human in authority often does not have the power to undo the damage that bad people do. But God is all-powerful. He can and will undo all the effects that wickedness has had on mankind. When God acts, he will do so in a way that will end evil forever! —Psalm 37:9-11.

## HOW DOES GOD FEEL ABOUT INJUSTICES WE FACE?

¹¹ In the meantime, how does God feel about what is going on in the world and in your life? Well, the Bible teaches that God is "a lover of justice." (Psalm 37:28) So he cares deeply about what is right and what is wrong. He hates all kinds of injustice. The Bible says that God "felt hurt at his heart" when badness filled the world in times past. (Genesis 6:5, 6) God has not changed. (Malachi 3:6) He still hates to see the suffering that is taking place worldwide. And God hates to see people suffer. "He cares for you," the Bible says.—1 Peter 5:7.

---

**11. (a) How does God feel about injustice? (b) How does God feel about your suffering?**

*What Is the Truth About God?*

13

¹² How can we be sure that God hates to see suffering? Here is further proof. The Bible teaches that man was made in the image of God. (Genesis 1:26) We thus have good qualities because God has good qualities. For example, does it bother you to see innocent people suffer? If you care about such injustices, be assured that God feels even more strongly about them.

¹³ One of the best things about humans is our ability to love. That also reflects God. The Bible teaches that "God is love." (1 John 4:8) We love because God loves. Would love move you to end the suffering and the injustice you see in the world? If you had the power to do that, would you do it? Of course you would! You can be just as sure that God will end suffering and injustice. The promises mentioned in the preface of this book are not mere dreams or idle hopes. God's promises are sure to come true! In order to put faith in such promises,

**12, 13. (a) Why do we have good qualities such as love, and how does love affect our view of the world? (b) Why can you be sure that God will really do something about world problems?**

though, you need to know more about the God who has made them.

## GOD WANTS YOU TO KNOW WHO HE IS

¹⁴ If you want someone to get to know you, what might you do? Would you not tell the person your name? Does God have a name? Many religions answer that his name is "God" or "Lord," but those are not personal names. They are titles, just as "king" and "president" are titles. The Bible teaches that God has many titles. "God" and "Lord" are among them. However, the Bible also teaches that God has a personal name: Jehovah. Psalm 83:18 says: "You, whose name is Jehovah, you alone are the Most High over all the earth." If your Bible translation does not contain that name, you may want to consult the Appendix on pages 248-51 of this book to learn why that is so. The truth is that God's name appears thousands of times in ancient Bible manuscripts. So Jehovah wants you to know his name and to use it. In a sense, he is using the Bible to introduce himself to you.

14. **What is God's name, and why should we use it?**

**15** God gave himself a name that is full of meaning. His name, Jehovah, means that God can fulfill any promise he makes and can carry out any purpose he has in mind.* God's name is unique, one of a kind. It belongs only to him. In a number of ways, Jehovah is unique. How is that so?

**16** We saw that Psalm 83:18 said of Jehovah: "You *alone* are the Most High." Similarly, Jehovah alone is referred to as "the Almighty." Revelation 15:3 says: "Great and wonderful are your works, Jehovah God, the Almighty. Righteous and true are your ways, King of eternity." The title "the Almighty" teaches us that Jehovah is the most powerful being there is. His power is unmatched; it is supreme. And the title "King of eternity" reminds us that Jehovah is unique in another sense. He alone has always existed. Psalm 90:2 says: "Even from time indefinite to time indefinite [or, forever] you are God." That thought inspires awe, does it not?

* There is more information on the meaning and the pronunciation of God's name in the Appendix on pages 248-51.

**15. What does the name Jehovah mean?**
**16, 17. What may we learn about Jehovah from the following titles: (a) "the Almighty"? (b) "King of eternity"? (c) "Creator"?**

*What Does the Bible Really Teach?*

**17** Jehovah is also unique in that he alone is the Creator. Revelation 4:11 reads: "You are worthy, Jehovah, even our God, to receive the glory and the honor and the power, because you created all things, and because of your will they existed and were created." Everything that you can think of —from the invisible spirit creatures in heaven to the stars that fill the night sky to the fruit that grows on the trees to the fish that swim in the oceans and rivers—all of it exists because Jehovah is the Creator!

## CAN YOU BE CLOSE TO JEHOVAH?

**18** Reading about Jehovah's awe-inspiring qualities makes some people feel a little uneasy. They fear that God is too high for them, that they could never get close to him or even matter to such a lofty God. But is this idea correct? The Bible teaches just the opposite. It says of Jehovah: "In fact, he is not far off from each one of us." (Acts 17:27) The Bible even urges us: "Draw close to God, and he will draw close to you."—James 4:8.

---

**18. Why do some people feel that they could never get close to God, but what does the Bible teach?**

**19** How can you draw close to God? To begin with, continue doing what you are doing now—learning about God. Jesus said: "This means everlasting life, their taking in knowledge of you, the only true God, and of the one whom you sent forth, Jesus Christ." (John 17:3) Yes, the Bible teaches that learning about Jehovah and Jesus leads to "everlasting life"! As already noted, "God is love." (1 John 4:16) Jehovah also has many other beautiful and appealing qualities. For example, the Bible says that Jehovah is "a God merciful and gracious, slow to anger and abundant in loving-kindness and truth." (Exodus 34:6) He is "good and ready to forgive." (Psalm 86:5) God is patient. (2 Peter 3:9) He is loyal. (Revelation 15:4) As you read more in the Bible, you will see how Jehovah has shown that he has these and many other appealing qualities.

**20** True, you cannot see God because he is an invisible spirit. (John 1:18; 4:24; 1 Timothy 1:17) By

---

**19. (a)** How can we begin to draw close to God, and with what benefit? **(b)** What qualities of God are most appealing to you?
**20-22. (a)** Does our inability to see God prevent us from getting close to him? Explain. **(b)** What may some well-meaning people urge you to do, but what should you do?

learning about him through the pages of the Bible, however, you can come to know him as a person. As the psalmist said, you can "behold the pleasantness of Jehovah." (Psalm 27:4; Romans 1:20) The more you learn about Jehovah, the more real he will become to you and the more reason you will have to love him and feel close to him.

21 You will come to understand why the Bible teaches us to think of Jehovah as our Father. (Matthew 6:9) Not only does our life come from him but he wants the best life possible for us—just as any loving father would want for his children. (Psalm 36:9) The Bible also teaches that humans can become Jehovah's friends. (James 2:23) Imagine—you can become a friend of the Creator of the universe!

22 As you learn more from the Bible, you may find that some well-meaning people will urge you to stop such studies. They may worry that you will change your beliefs. But do not let anyone stop you from forming the best friendship you can ever have.

23 Of course, there will be things that you do not

23, 24. (a) Why should you continue to ask questions about what you are learning? (b) What is the subject of the next chapter?

*What Is the Truth About God?*

19

understand at first. It can be a little humbling to ask for help, but do not hold back because of embarrassment. Jesus said that it is good to be humble, like a little child. (Matthew 18:2-4) And children, as we know, ask a lot of questions. God wants you to find the answers. The Bible praises some who were eager to learn about God. They checked carefully in the Scriptures to make sure that what they were learning was the truth.—Acts 17:11.

[24] The best way to learn about Jehovah is to examine the Bible. It is different from any other book. In what way? The next chapter will consider that subject.

---

## WHAT THE BIBLE TEACHES

- God cares about you personally.—1 Peter 5:7.
- God's personal name is Jehovah.
  —Psalm 83:18.
- Jehovah invites you to draw close to him.
  —James 4:8.
- Jehovah is loving, kind, and merciful.
  —Exodus 34:6; 1 John 4:8, 16.

---

# CHAPTER TWO

# The Bible—A Book From God

**In what ways is the Bible different from any other book?**

**How can the Bible help you cope with personal problems?**

**Why can you trust the prophecies recorded in the Bible?**

CAN you recall a time when you received a fine gift from a dear friend? Likely, the experience was not only exciting but also heartwarming. After all, a gift tells you something about the giver—that he or she values your friendship. No doubt you expressed gratitude for your friend's thoughtful gift.

² The Bible is a gift from God, one for which we can be truly grateful. This unique book reveals things that we could never find out otherwise. For example, it tells us about the creation of the starry heavens, the earth, and the first man and woman. The Bible contains reliable principles to help us cope with life's

1, 2. In what ways is the Bible an exciting gift from God?

problems and anxieties. It explains how God will fulfill his purpose and bring about better conditions on the earth. What an exciting gift the Bible is!

3 The Bible is also a heartwarming gift, for it reveals something about the Giver, Jehovah God. The fact that he has provided such a book is proof that he wants us to get to know him well. Indeed, the Bible can help you to draw close to Jehovah.

4 If you have a copy of the Bible, you are far from alone. In whole or in part, the Bible has been published in more than 2,300 languages and thus is available to more than 90 percent of the world's population. On the average, more than a million Bibles are distributed *each week!* Billions of copies of either the whole Bible or part of it have been produced. Surely, there is no other book like the Bible.

5 Furthermore, the Bible "is inspired of God." (2 Timothy 3:16) In what way? The Bible itself answers: "Men spoke from God as they were borne

3. What does the provision of the Bible tell us about Jehovah, and why is this heartwarming?
4. What impresses you about the distribution of the Bible?
5. In what way is the Bible "inspired of God"?

*What Does the Bible Really Teach?*

along by holy spirit." (2 Peter 1:21) To illustrate: A businessman might have a secretary write a letter. That letter contains the businessman's thoughts and instructions. Hence, it is really *his* letter, not the secretary's. In a similar way, the Bible contains God's message, not that of the men who wrote it down. Thus, the entire Bible truthfully is "the word of God."—1 Thessalonians 2:13.

## HARMONIOUS AND ACCURATE

⁶ The Bible was written over a 1,600-year period. Its writers lived at different times and came from many walks of life. Some were farmers, fishermen, and shepherds. Others were prophets, judges, and kings. The Gospel writer Luke was a doctor. Despite the varied backgrounds of its writers, the Bible is harmonious from beginning to end.*

⁷ The first book of the Bible tells us how mankind's problems began. The last book shows that the whole

---

* Although some people say that certain parts of the Bible contradict other parts of it, such claims are unfounded. See chapter 7 of the book *The Bible—God's Word or Man's?* published by Jehovah's Witnesses.

**6, 7. Why is the harmony of the material in the Bible particularly noteworthy?**

earth will become a paradise, or garden. All the material in the Bible covers thousands of years of history and relates in some way to the unfolding of God's purpose. The harmony of the Bible is impressive, but that is what we would expect of a book from God.

⁸ The Bible is scientifically accurate. It even contains information that was far ahead of its time. For example, the book of Leviticus contained laws for ancient Israel on quarantine and hygiene when surrounding nations knew nothing about such matters. At a time when there were wrong ideas about the shape of the earth, the Bible referred to it as a circle, or sphere. (Isaiah 40:22) The Bible accurately said that the earth 'hangs on nothing.' (Job 26:7) Of course, the Bible is not a science textbook. But when it touches on scientific matters, it is accurate. Is this not what we would expect of a book from God?

⁹ The Bible is also historically accurate and reliable. Its accounts are specific. They include not only the

8. Give examples showing that the Bible is scientifically accurate.
9. (a) In what ways does the Bible show itself to be historically accurate and reliable? (b) What does the honesty of its writers tell you about the Bible?

*What Does the Bible Really Teach?*

names but also the ancestry of individuals.* In contrast to secular historians, who often do not mention the defeats of their own people, Bible writers were honest, even recording their own failings and those of their nation. In the Bible book of Numbers, for instance, the writer Moses admits his own serious error for which he was severely reproved. (Numbers 20:2-12) Such honesty is rare in other historical accounts but is found in the Bible because it is a book from God.

## A BOOK OF PRACTICAL WISDOM

¹⁰ Because the Bible is inspired of God, it is "beneficial for teaching, for reproving, for setting things straight." (2 Timothy 3:16) Yes, the Bible is a practical book. It reflects a keen understanding of human nature. No wonder, for its Author, Jehovah God, is the Creator! He understands our thinking and emotions better than we do. Furthermore, Jehovah knows what we need in order to be happy. He also knows what pathways we should avoid.

* For example, note the detailed ancestral line of Jesus set out at Luke 3:23-38.

**10. Why is it not surprising that the Bible is a practical book?**

¹¹ Consider Jesus' speech called the Sermon on the Mount, recorded in Matthew chapters 5 to 7. In this masterpiece of teaching, Jesus spoke on a number of topics, including the way to find true happiness, how to settle disputes, how to pray, and how to have the proper view of material things. Jesus' words are just as powerful and practical today as they were when he spoke them.

¹² Some Bible principles deal with family life, work habits, and relationships with others. The Bible's principles apply to all people, and its counsel is always beneficial. The wisdom found in the Bible is summarized by God's words through the prophet Isaiah: "I, Jehovah, am your God, the One teaching you to benefit yourself."—Isaiah 48:17.

## A BOOK OF PROPHECY

¹³ The Bible contains numerous prophecies, many of which have already been fulfilled. Consider an ex-

11, 12. (a) What topics did Jesus discuss in his Sermon on the Mount? (b) What other practical matters are considered in the Bible, and why is its counsel timeless?

13. What details did Jehovah inspire the prophet Isaiah to record regarding Babylon?

*What Does the Bible Really Teach?*

ample. Through the prophet Isaiah, who lived in the eighth century B.C.E., Jehovah foretold that the city of Babylon would be destroyed. (Isaiah 13:19; 14:22, 23) Details were given to show just *how* this would happen. Invading armies would dry up Babylon's river and march into the city without a battle. That is not all. Isaiah's prophecy even named the king who would conquer Babylon—Cyrus.—Isaiah 44:27–45:2.

¹⁴ Some 200 years later—on the night of October 5/6, 539 B.C.E.—an army encamped near Babylon. Who was its commander? A Persian king named Cyrus. The stage was thus set for the fulfillment of an amazing prophecy. But would the army of Cyrus invade Babylon without a battle, as foretold?

¹⁵ The Babylonians were holding a festival that night and felt secure behind their massive city walls. Meanwhile, Cyrus cleverly diverted the water of the river that flowed through the city. Soon the water was shallow enough for his men to cross the riverbed and approach the walls of the city. But how would Cyrus' army get past Babylon's walls? For some reason, on

**14, 15. How were some details of Isaiah's prophecy about Babylon fulfilled?**

that night the doors to the city were carelessly left open!

16 Regarding Babylon, it was foretold: "She will never be inhabited, nor will she reside for generation after generation. And there the Arab will not pitch his tent, and no shepherds will let their flocks lie down there." (Isaiah 13:20) This prophecy did more than predict a city's fall. It showed that Babylon would be desolated *permanently*. You can see evidence of the fulfillment of these words. The uninhabited site of ancient Babylon—about 50 miles south of Baghdad, Iraq—is proof that what Jehovah spoke through Isaiah has been fulfilled: "I will sweep her with the broom of annihilation."—Isaiah 14:22, 23.*

17 Considering how the Bible is a book of reliable prophecy is faith strengthening, is it not? After all, if Jehovah God has fulfilled his past promises, we have every reason to be confident that he will also fulfill his promise of a paradise earth. (Numbers 23:19) In-

* For more information on Bible prophecy, see pages 27-9 of the brochure *A Book for All People,* published by Jehovah's Witnesses.

16. (a) What did Isaiah foretell about the final outcome of Babylon? (b) How was Isaiah's prophecy about Babylon's desolation fulfilled?
17. How is the fulfillment of Bible prophecy faith strengthening?

*What Does the Bible Really Teach?*

deed, we have "hope of the everlasting life which God, who cannot lie, promised before times long lasting."—Titus 1:2.*

## "THE WORD OF GOD IS ALIVE"

[18] From what we have considered in this chapter, it is clear that the Bible is truly a unique book. Yet, its value extends far beyond its internal harmony, scientific and historical accuracy, practical wisdom, and reliable prophecy. The Christian apostle Paul wrote: "The word of God is alive and exerts power and is sharper than any two-edged sword and pierces even to the dividing of soul and spirit, and of joints and their marrow, and is able to discern thoughts and intentions of the heart."—Hebrews 4:12.

[19] Reading God's "word," or message, in the Bible

* The destruction of Babylon is just one example of fulfilled Bible prophecy. Other examples include the destruction of Tyre and Nineveh. (Ezekiel 26:1-5; Zephaniah 2:13-15) Also, Daniel's prophecy foretold a succession of world empires that would come into power after Babylon. These included Medo-Persia and Greece. (Daniel 8:5-7, 20-22) See the Appendix, pages 254-6, for a discussion of the many Messianic prophecies that were fulfilled in Jesus Christ.

**18. What powerful statement does the Christian apostle Paul make about "the word of God"?**
**19, 20. (a) How can the Bible help you to examine yourself? (b) How can you show your gratitude for God's unique gift, the Bible?**

can change our life. It can help us to examine ourselves as never before. We may claim to love God, but how we react to what his inspired Word, the Bible, teaches will reveal our true thoughts, even the very intentions of the heart.

[20] The Bible truly is a book from God. It is a book that is to be read, studied, and loved. Show your gratitude for this divine gift by continuing to peer into its contents. As you do so, you will gain a deep appreciation of God's purpose for mankind. Just what that purpose is and how it will be realized will be discussed in the following chapter.

---

### WHAT THE BIBLE TEACHES

- The Bible is inspired of God and thus is accurate and reliable.—2 Timothy 3:16.

- The information found in God's Word is practical for everyday life.—Isaiah 48:17.

- God's promises found in the Bible are certain to be fulfilled.—Numbers 23:19.

---

*What Does the Bible Really Teach?*

# CHAPTER THREE

# What Is God's Purpose for the Earth?

**What is God's purpose for mankind?**

**How has God been challenged?**

**What will life on earth be like in the future?**

GOD'S purpose for the earth is really wonderful. Jehovah wants the earth to be filled with happy, healthy people. The Bible says that "God planted a garden in Eden" and that he "made to grow . . . every tree desirable to one's sight and good for food." After God created the first man and woman, Adam and Eve, He put them in that lovely home and told them: "Be fruitful and become many and fill the earth and subdue it." (Genesis 1:28; 2:8, 9, 15) So it was God's purpose that humans have children, extend the boundaries of that garden home earth wide, and take care of the animals.

² Do you think that Jehovah God's purpose for

---

1. What is God's purpose for the earth?
2. (a) How do we know that God's purpose for the earth will be fulfilled? (b) What does the Bible say about humans living forever?

people to live in an earthly paradise will ever be realized? "I have even spoken it," God declares, "I shall also do it." (Isaiah 46:9-11; 55:11) Yes, what God purposes he will surely do! He says that he "did not create [the earth] simply for nothing" but "formed it even to be inhabited." (Isaiah 45:18) What kind of people did God want to live on the earth? And for how long did he want them to live here? The Bible answers: "The *righteous* themselves will possess the earth, and they will *reside forever upon it.*"—Psalm 37:29; Revelation 21: 3, 4.

³ Obviously, this has not happened yet. People now get sick and die; they even fight and kill one another. Something went wrong. Surely, however, God did not purpose that the earth should be as we see it today! What happened? Why has God's purpose not been fulfilled? No history book written by man can tell us because the trouble started in heaven.

**3. What sad conditions now exist on earth, and what questions does this raise?**

*What Does the Bible Really Teach?*

# THE ORIGIN OF AN ENEMY

⁴ The first book of the Bible tells of an opposer of God who showed up in the garden of Eden. He is described as "the serpent," but he was not a mere animal. The last book of the Bible identifies him as "the one called Devil and Satan, who is misleading the entire inhabited earth." He is also called "the *original* serpent." (Genesis 3:1; Revelation 12:9) This powerful angel, or invisible spirit creature, used a serpent to speak to Eve, even as a skilled person can make it seem that his voice is coming from a nearby doll or dummy. That spirit person had no doubt been present when God prepared the earth for humans.—Job 38:4, 7.

⁵ Since all of Jehovah's creations are perfect, however, who made this "Devil," this "Satan"? Put simply, *one of the powerful spirit sons of God turned himself into the Devil.* How was this possible? Well, today a person who was once decent and honest may become a thief. How does that happen? The

4, 5. (a) Who actually spoke to Eve by means of a serpent? (b) How might a formerly decent, honest person become a thief?

person may allow a wrong desire to develop in his heart. If he *keeps thinking about it,* that wrong desire may become very strong. Then if the opportunity presents itself, he may act upon the bad desire that he has been thinking about.—James 1:13-15.

6 This happened in the case of Satan the Devil. He apparently heard God tell Adam and Eve to have children and to fill the earth with their offspring. (Genesis 1:27, 28) 'Why, all these humans could worship me rather than God!' Satan evidently thought. So a wrong desire built up in his heart. Eventually, he took action to deceive Eve by telling her lies about God. (Genesis 3:1-5) He thus became a "Devil," which means "Slanderer." At the same time, he became "Satan," which means "Opposer."

7 By using lies and trickery, Satan the Devil caused Adam and Eve to disobey God. (Genesis 2: 17; 3:6) As a result, they eventually died, as God had said they would if they disobeyed. (Genesis 3:17-19) Since Adam became imperfect when he

6. How did a powerful spirit son of God become Satan the Devil?
7. (a) Why did Adam and Eve die? (b) Why do all of Adam's offspring grow old and die?

*What Does the Bible Really Teach?*

sinned, all his offspring inherited sin from him. (Romans 5:12) The situation might be illustrated with a pan used for baking bread. If the pan has a dent in it, what happens to each loaf of bread made in the pan? Each loaf has a dent, or an imperfection, in it. Similarly, each human has inherited a "dent" of imperfection from Adam. That is why all humans grow old and die.—Romans 3:23.

⁸ When Satan led Adam and Eve into sinning against God, he was really leading a rebellion. He was challenging Jehovah's way of ruling. In effect, Satan was saying: 'God is a bad ruler. He tells lies and holds back good things from his subjects. Humans do not need to have God ruling over them. They can decide for themselves what is good and what is bad. And they will be better off under my rulership.' How would God handle such an insulting challenge? Some think that God should simply have put the rebels to death. But would that have answered Satan's challenge? Would it have proved that God's way of ruling is right?

8, 9. (a) **What challenge did Satan evidently make? (b) Why did God not destroy the rebels immediately?**

⁹ Jehovah's perfect sense of justice would not allow him to put the rebels to death right away. He decided that time was needed to answer Satan's challenge in a satisfying way and to prove that the Devil is a liar. So God determined that he would permit humans to rule themselves for some time under Satan's influence. Why Jehovah did that and why he has allowed so much time to pass before settling these issues will be discussed in Chapter 11 of this book. Now, though, it is good to think about this: Were Adam and Eve right to believe Satan, who had never done anything good for them? Was it right for them to believe that Jehovah, who had given them everything they had, is a cruel liar? What would you have done?

¹⁰ It is good to think about these questions because each of us faces similar issues today. Yes, you have the opportunity to support Jehovah's side in answer to Satan's challenge. You can accept Jehovah as your Ruler and help to show that Satan is a

**10. How can you support Jehovah's side in answer to Satan's challenge?**

liar. (Psalm 73:28; Proverbs 27:11) Sadly, only a few among the billions of people in this world make such a choice. This raises an important question, Does the Bible really teach that Satan rules this world?

## WHO RULES THIS WORLD?

11 Jesus never doubted that Satan is the ruler of this world. In some miraculous way, Satan once showed Jesus "all the kingdoms of the world and their glory." Satan then promised Jesus: "All these things I will give you if you fall down and do an act of worship to me." (Matthew 4:8, 9; Luke 4:5, 6) Think about this. Would that offer have been a *temptation* to Jesus if Satan was not the ruler of these kingdoms? Jesus did not deny that all these worldly governments were Satan's. Surely, Jesus would have done that if Satan was not the power behind them.

12 Of course, Jehovah is the Almighty God, the Creator of the marvelous universe. (Revelation 4:11)

---

**11, 12. (a) How does a temptation of Jesus reveal that Satan is the ruler of this world? (b) What else proves that Satan is the ruler of this world?**

Refer us to Noah 2 Peter 3:3-7

Yet, nowhere does the Bible say that either Jehovah God or Jesus Christ is ruler of this world. In fact, Jesus specifically referred to Satan as "the ruler of this world." (John 12:31; 14:30; 16:11) The Bible even refers to Satan the Devil as "the god of this system of things." (2 Corinthians 4:3, 4) Regarding this opposer, or Satan, the Christian apostle John wrote: "The whole world is lying in the power of the wicked one."—1 John 5:19.

## HOW SATAN'S WORLD WILL BE REMOVED

¹³ With each passing year, the world is becoming more and more dangerous. It is overrun with warring armies, dishonest politicians, hypocritical religious leaders, and hardened criminals. The world as a whole is beyond reform. The Bible reveals that the time is near when God will eliminate the wicked world during his war of Armageddon. This will make way for a righteous new world.—Revelation 16:14-16.

¹⁴ Jehovah God selected Jesus Christ to be Ruler

13. Why is there a need for a new world?
14. Whom has God selected to be Ruler of His Kingdom, and how was this foretold?

of His heavenly Kingdom, or government. Long ago, the Bible foretold: "Unto us a child is born, unto us a son is given: and the government shall be upon his shoulder: and his name shall be called . . . Prince of Peace. Of the increase of his government and peace there shall be no end." (Isaiah 9:6, 7, *King James Version*) Regarding this government, Jesus taught his followers to pray: "Let your kingdom come. Let your will take place, as in heaven, also upon earth." (Matthew 6:10) As we will see later in this book, God's Kingdom will soon remove all the governments of this world, and it itself will replace all of them. (Daniel 2:44) Then God's Kingdom will usher in an earthly paradise.

## A NEW WORLD IS AT HAND!

15 The Bible assures us: "There are new heavens and a new earth that we are awaiting according to [God's] promise, and in these righteousness is to dwell." (2 Peter 3:13; Isaiah 65:17) Sometimes when the Bible speaks of "the earth," it means the people who live on the earth. (Genesis 11:1) So the

**15. What is the "new earth"?**

righteous "new earth" is a society of people who receive God's approval.

¹⁶ Jesus promised that in the coming new world, those approved by God would receive the gift of "everlasting life." (Mark 10:30) Please open your Bible to John 3:16 and 17:3, and read what Jesus said we must do to receive everlasting life. Now consider from the Bible the blessings that will be enjoyed by those who qualify for that wonderful gift from God in the coming earthly Paradise.

¹⁷ *Wickedness, warfare, crime, and violence will be gone.* "The wicked one will be no more . . . But the meek ones themselves will possess the earth." (Psalm 37:10, 11) Peace will exist because 'God will make wars cease to the ends of the earth.' (Psalm 46:9; Isaiah 2:4) Then "the righteous one will sprout, and the abundance of peace until the moon is no more"—and that means forever!—Psalm 72:7.

---

**16. What is a priceless gift from God to those whom he approves, and what must we do to receive it?**

**17, 18. How can we be sure that there will be peace and security everywhere on earth?**

*What Does the Bible Really Teach?*

**18** *Jehovah's worshipers will live in security.* As long as the Israelites in Bible times obeyed God, they lived in security. (Leviticus 25:18, 19) How wonderful it will be to enjoy similar security in Paradise! —Isaiah 32:18; Micah 4:4.

**19** *Food shortages will not exist.* "There will come to be plenty of grain on the earth," sang the psalmist. "On the top of the mountains there will be an overflow." (Psalm 72:16) Jehovah God will bless his righteous ones, and "the earth itself will certainly give its produce."—Psalm 67:6.

**20** *The whole earth will become a paradise.* Lovely new homes and gardens will occupy land that had once been ruined by sinful humans. (Isaiah 65:21-24; Revelation 11:18) As time passes, parts of the earth already subdued will expand until the whole globe is as beautiful and productive as the garden of Eden. And God will never fail to 'open his hand and satisfy the desire of every living thing.'—Psalm 145:16.

---

**19.** Why do we know that food will be abundant in God's new world?
**20.** Why can we be sure that the whole earth will become a paradise?

**21** *There will be peace between humans and animals.* Wild and domestic animals will feed together. Even a little child will have nothing to fear from animals that are now dangerous.—Isaiah 11:6-9; 65:25.

**22** *Sickness will vanish.* As Ruler of God's heavenly Kingdom, Jesus will do healing on a far grander scale than when he was on earth. (Matthew 9:35; Mark 1:40-42; John 5:5-9) Then "no resident will say: 'I am sick.'"—Isaiah 33:24; 35:5, 6.

**23** *Dead loved ones will be restored to life with the prospect of never dying.* All those sleeping in death who are in God's memory will be brought back to life. In fact, "there is going to be a resurrection of both the righteous and the unrighteous."—Acts 24: 15; John 5:28, 29.

*resurrection of damnation?*

**24** What a marvelous future awaits those who choose to learn about our Grand Creator, Jehovah God, and to serve him! It was to the coming Paradise on earth that Jesus pointed when he prom-

21. What shows that peace will exist between humans and animals?
22. What will happen to sickness?
23. Why will the resurrection bring joy to our hearts?
24. How do you feel about living in Paradise on earth?

*What Does the Bible Really Teach?*

ised the evildoer who died alongside him: "You will be with me in Paradise." (Luke 23:43) It is vital that we learn more about Jesus Christ, through whom all these blessings will be made possible.

---

## WHAT THE BIBLE TEACHES

- God's purpose to make the earth a paradise will be fulfilled.—Isaiah 45:18; 55:11.

- Satan now rules this world.—John 12:31; 1 John 5:19.

- In the coming new world, God will bestow many blessings on mankind. —Psalm 37:10, 11, 29.

---

# CHAPTER FOUR

# Who Is Jesus Christ?

**What is Jesus' special role?**

**Where did he come from?**

**What kind of person was he?**

THERE are many famous people in the world. Some are well-known in their own community, city, or country. Others are known worldwide. However, just knowing the name of someone famous does not mean that you truly *know* him. It does not mean that you know details about his background and what he is really like as a person.

[2] People around the world have heard something about Jesus Christ, even though he lived on earth some 2,000 years ago. Yet, many are confused about who Jesus really was. Some say that he was merely a good man. Others claim that he was nothing more

**1, 2. (a) Why does knowing about someone famous not mean that you truly *know* him? (b) What confusion is there about Jesus?**

*What Does the Bible Really Teach?*

than a prophet. Still others believe that Jesus is God and should be worshiped. Should he?

3 It is important for you to know the truth about Jesus. Why? Because the Bible says: "This means everlasting life, their taking in knowledge of you, the only true God, *and of the one whom you sent forth, Jesus Christ.*" (John 17:3) Yes, knowing the truth about Jehovah God and about Jesus Christ can lead to everlasting life on a paradise earth. (John 14:6) Furthermore, Jesus sets the best example of how to live and how to treat others. (John 13: 34, 35) In the first chapter of this book, we discussed the truth about God. Now let us consider what the Bible really teaches about Jesus Christ.

## THE PROMISED MESSIAH

4 Long before Jesus was born, the Bible foretold the coming of the one whom God would send as the Messiah, or Christ. The titles "Messiah" (from a Hebrew word) and "Christ" (from a Greek word) both mean "Anointed One." This promised One would be anointed, that is, appointed by God to a

3. Why is it important for you to know the truth about Jesus?
4. What do the titles "Messiah" and "Christ" mean?

*Who Is Jesus Christ?*

special position. In later chapters of this book, we will learn more about the Messiah's important place in the fulfillment of God's promises. We will also learn about the blessings that Jesus can bring us even now. Before Jesus was born, however, many no doubt wondered, 'Who will prove to be the Messiah?'

5 In the first century C.E., the disciples of Jesus of Nazareth were fully convinced that he was the foretold Messiah. (John 1:41) One of the disciples, a man named Simon Peter, openly said to Jesus: "You are the Christ." (Matthew 16:16) How, though, could those disciples—and how can we—be sure that Jesus really is the promised Messiah?

6 The prophets of God who lived before Jesus foretold many details about the Messiah. These details would help others to identify him. We might illustrate things this way: Suppose you were asked to go to a busy bus depot or a train station or an airport to pick up someone you had never met before.

**5.** Of what were the disciples of Jesus fully convinced regarding him?
**6.** Illustrate how Jehovah has helped faithful ones to identify the Messiah.

*What Does the Bible Really Teach?*

Would it not help if someone gave you a few details about him? Similarly, by means of the Bible prophets, Jehovah gave a rather detailed description of what the Messiah would do and what he would experience. The fulfillment of these many prophecies would help faithful ones to identify him clearly.

⁷ Consider just two examples. First, over 700 years in advance, the prophet Micah foretold that the promised One would be born in Bethlehem, a small town in the land of Judah. (Micah 5:2) Where was Jesus actually born? Why, in that very town! (Matthew 2:1, 3-9) Second, many centuries in advance, the prophecy recorded at Daniel 9:25 pointed to the very year when the Messiah was to appear—29 C.E.* The fulfillment of these and other prophecies proves that Jesus was the promised Messiah.

⁸ Further proof that Jesus was the Messiah became clear near the end of 29 C.E. That is the

* For an explanation of Daniel's prophecy fulfilled in connection with Jesus, see the Appendix, pages 252-4.

7. What are two of the prophecies that were fulfilled in connection with Jesus?
8, 9. What proof that Jesus was the Messiah became clear at his baptism?

year when Jesus went to John the Baptizer to be baptized in the Jordan River. Jehovah had promised John a sign so that he could identify the Messiah. John saw that sign at Jesus' baptism. The Bible says that this is what happened: "After being baptized Jesus immediately came up from the water; and, look! the heavens were opened up, and he saw descending like a dove God's spirit coming upon him. Look! Also, there was a voice from the heavens that said: 'This is my Son, the beloved, whom I have approved.'" (Matthew 3:16, 17) After seeing and hearing what happened, John had no doubt that Jesus was sent by God. (John 1:32-34) At the moment when God's spirit, or active force, was poured out upon him that day, Jesus became the Messiah, or Christ, the one appointed to be Leader and King.—Isaiah 55:4.

⁹ The fulfillment of Bible prophecy and Jehovah God's own testimony plainly show that Jesus was the promised Messiah. But the Bible answers two other important questions about Jesus Christ: Where did he come from, and what kind of person was he?

# WHERE DID JESUS COME FROM?

¹⁰ The Bible teaches that Jesus lived in heaven before he came to earth. Micah prophesied that the Messiah would be born in Bethlehem and also said that His origin was "from early times." (Micah 5:2) On many occasions, Jesus himself said that he lived in heaven before being born as a human. (John 3: 13; 6:38, 62; 17:4, 5) As a spirit creature in heaven, Jesus had a special relationship with Jehovah.

¹¹ Jesus is Jehovah's most precious Son—and for good reason. He is called "the firstborn of all creation," for he was God's first creation.* (Colossians 1:15) There is something else that makes this Son special. He is the "only-begotten Son." (John 3:16) This means that Jesus is the only one directly created by God. Jesus is also the only one whom God used when He created all other things. (Colossians

---

* Jehovah is called a Father because he is the Creator. (Isaiah 64:8) Since Jesus was created by God, he is called God's Son. For similar reasons, other spirit creatures and even the man Adam are called sons of God.—Job 1:6; Luke 3:38.

---

**10.** What does the Bible teach about Jesus' existence before he came to earth?

**11.** How does the Bible show that Jesus is Jehovah's most precious Son?

1:16) Then, too, Jesus is called "the Word." (John 1:14) This tells us that he spoke for God, no doubt delivering messages and instructions to the Father's other sons, both spirit and human.

¹² Is the firstborn Son equal to God, as some believe? That is not what the Bible teaches. As we noted in the preceding paragraph, the Son was created. Obviously, then, he had a beginning, whereas Jehovah God has no beginning or end. (Psalm 90:2) The only-begotten Son never even considered trying to be equal to his Father. The Bible clearly teaches that the Father is greater than the Son. (John 14:28; 1 Corinthians 11:3) Jehovah alone is "God Almighty." (Genesis 17:1) Therefore, he has no equal.*

¹³ Jehovah and his firstborn Son enjoyed close association for billions of years—long before the starry heavens and the earth were created. How they must have loved each other! (John 3:35; 14:31) This

* For further proof that the firstborn Son is not equal to God, see the Appendix, pages 257-60.

**12. How do we know that the firstborn Son is not equal to God?**
**13. What does the Bible mean when it refers to the Son as "the image of the invisible God"?**

*What Does the Bible Really Teach?*

dear Son was just like his Father. That is why the Bible refers to the Son as "the image of the invisible God." (Colossians 1:15) Yes, even as a human son may closely resemble his father in various ways, this heavenly Son reflected his Father's qualities and personality.

14 Jehovah's only-begotten Son willingly left heaven and came down to earth to live as a human. But you may wonder, 'How was it possible for a spirit creature to be born as a human?' To accomplish this, Jehovah performed a miracle. He transferred the life of his firstborn Son from heaven to the womb of a Jewish virgin named Mary. No human father was involved. Mary thus gave birth to a perfect son and named him Jesus.—Luke 1:30-35.

## WHAT KIND OF PERSON WAS JESUS?

15 What Jesus said and did while on earth helps us to get to know him well. More than that, through Jesus we come to know Jehovah better. Why is this the case? Recall that this Son is a perfect reflection

14. How did Jehovah's only-begotten Son come to be born as a human?
15. Why can we say that through Jesus we come to know Jehovah better?

of his Father. That is why Jesus told one of his disciples: "He that has seen me has seen the Father also." (John 14:9) The four Bible books known as the Gospels—Matthew, Mark, Luke, and John—tell us much about the life, activity, and personal qualities of Jesus Christ.

¹⁶ Jesus was well-known as "Teacher." (John 1:38; 13:13) What did he teach? Primarily, his message was "the good news of the kingdom"—that is, God's Kingdom, the heavenly government that will rule over the entire earth and will bring endless blessings to obedient humans. (Matthew 4:23) Whose message was this? Jesus himself said: "What I teach is not mine, but belongs to him that sent me," namely, Jehovah. (John 7:16) Jesus knew that his Father wants humans to hear about the good news of the Kingdom. In Chapter 8, we will learn more about God's Kingdom and what it will accomplish.

¹⁷ Where did Jesus do his teaching? Everywhere he found people—in the countryside as well as in

16. What was Jesus' primary message, and where did his teachings come from?
17. Where did Jesus do his teaching, and why did he go to great lengths to teach others?

*What Does the Bible Really Teach?*

cities, in villages, in marketplaces, and in their homes. Jesus did not expect people to come to him. He went to them. (Mark 6:56; Luke 19:5, 6) Why did Jesus go to such lengths and spend so much of his time preaching and teaching? Because doing so was God's will for him. Jesus always did his Father's will. (John 8:28, 29) But there was another reason why he preached. He felt compassion for the crowds of people who came out to see him. (Matthew 9:35, 36) They were neglected by their religious leaders, who should have been teaching them the truth about God and his purposes. Jesus knew how much the people needed to hear the Kingdom message.

18 Jesus was a man of tender warmth and deep feelings. Others thus found him to be approachable and kind. Even children felt at ease with him. (Mark 10:13-16) Jesus was impartial. He hated corruption and injustice. (Matthew 21:12, 13) At a time when women received little respect and had few privileges, he treated them with dignity. (John 4:9, 27)

18. What qualities of Jesus do you find most appealing?

Jesus was genuinely humble. On one occasion, he washed the feet of his apostles, a service usually performed by a lowly servant.

[19] Jesus was sensitive to the needs of others. This was especially evident when, under the power of God's spirit, he performed miracles of healing. (Matthew 14:14) For example, a man with leprosy came to Jesus and said: "If you just want to, you can make me clean." Jesus personally felt this man's pain and suffering. Moved with pity, Jesus stretched out his hand and touched the man, saying: "I want to. Be made clean." And the sick man was healed! (Mark 1:40-42) Can you imagine how that man must have felt?

## FAITHFUL TO THE END

[20] Jesus set the finest example of loyal obedience to God. He remained faithful to his heavenly Father under all kinds of circumstances and despite all types of opposition and suffering. Jesus firmly and

19. What example shows that Jesus was sensitive to the needs of others?

20, 21. How did Jesus set an example of loyal obedience to God?

successfully resisted Satan's temptations. (Matthew 4:1-11) At one time, some of Jesus' own relatives did not put faith in him, even saying that he was "out of his mind." (Mark 3:21) But Jesus did not let them influence him; he kept right on doing God's work. Despite insults and abuse, Jesus maintained self-control, never trying to harm his opposers. —1 Peter 2:21-23.

21 Jesus remained faithful until death—a cruel and painful death at the hands of his enemies. (Philippians 2:8) Consider what he endured on the last day of his life as a human. He was arrested, accused by false witnesses, convicted by corrupt judges, laughed at by mobs, and tortured by soldiers. Nailed to a stake, he took his last breath, crying out: "It has been accomplished!" (John 19:30) However, on the third day after Jesus died, his heavenly Father resurrected him back to spirit life. (1 Peter 3:18) A few weeks later, he returned to heaven. There, he "sat down at the right hand of God" and waited to receive kingly power.—Hebrews 10:12, 13.

[22] What did Jesus accomplish by remaining faithful until death? Jesus' death actually opens to us the opportunity for eternal life on a paradise earth, in harmony with Jehovah's original purpose. How Jesus' death makes that possible will be discussed in the next chapter.

---

22. What did Jesus accomplish by remaining faithful until death?

*7·29*

---

### WHAT THE BIBLE TEACHES

- Fulfilled prophecy and God's own testimony prove that Jesus is the Messiah, or Christ. —Matthew 16:16.

- Jesus lived in heaven as a spirit creature long before he came to earth.—John 3:13.

- Jesus was a teacher, a man of tender warmth, and an example of perfect obedience to God. —Matthew 9:35, 36.

---

*What Does the Bible Really Teach?*

# CHAPTER FIVE

# The Ransom—God's Greatest Gift

### What is the ransom?

### How was it provided?

### What can it mean for you?

### How can you show that you appreciate it?

WHAT is the greatest gift you have ever received? A gift does not have to be expensive to be important. After all, the true value of a gift is not necessarily measured in terms of money. Rather, when a gift brings you happiness or fills a real need in your life, it has great value to you personally.

² Of the many gifts you could ever hope to receive, there is one that stands out above all others. It is a gift from God to mankind. Jehovah has given us many things, but his greatest gift to us is the ransom sacrifice of his Son, Jesus Christ. (Matthew

---

1, 2. (a) When does a gift have great value to you personally? (b) Why can it be said that the ransom is the most valuable gift you could ever receive?

20:28) As we will see in this chapter, the ransom is the most valuable gift you could possibly receive, for it can bring you untold happiness and can fill your most important needs. The ransom is really the greatest expression of Jehovah's love for you.

## WHAT IS THE RANSOM?

³ Put simply, the ransom is Jehovah's means to deliver, or save, humankind from sin and death. (Ephesians 1:7) To grasp the meaning of this Bible teaching, we need to think back to what happened in the garden of Eden. Only if we understand what Adam lost when he sinned can we appreciate why the ransom is such a valuable gift to us.

⁴ When he created Adam, Jehovah gave him something truly precious—perfect human life. Consider what that meant for Adam. Made with a perfect body and mind, he would never get sick, grow old, or die. As a perfect human, he had a special relationship with Jehovah. The Bible says that Adam was a "son of God." (Luke 3:38) So Adam enjoyed

---

3. What is the ransom, and what do we need to understand in order to appreciate this valuable gift?
4. What did perfect human life mean for Adam?

*What Does the Bible Really Teach?*

a close relationship with Jehovah God, like that of a son with a loving father. Jehovah communicated with his earthly son, giving Adam satisfying assignments of work and letting him know what was expected of him.—Genesis 1:28-30; 2:16, 17.

[5] Adam was made "in God's image." (Genesis 1:27) That did not mean that Adam resembled God in appearance. As we learned in Chapter 1 of this book, Jehovah is an invisible spirit. (John 4:24) So Jehovah does not have a body of flesh and blood. Being made in God's image meant that Adam was created with qualities like those of God, including love, wisdom, justice, and power. Adam was like his Father in another important way in that he possessed free will. Hence, Adam was not like a machine that can perform only what it is designed or programmed to do. Instead, he could make personal decisions, choosing between right and wrong. If he had chosen to obey God, he would have lived forever in Paradise on earth.

5. What does the Bible mean when it says that Adam was made "in God's image"?

⁶ Clearly, then, when Adam disobeyed God and was condemned to death, he paid a very high price. His sin cost him his perfect human life with all its blessings. (Genesis 3:17-19) Sadly, Adam lost this precious life not only for himself but also for his future offspring. God's Word says: "Through one man [Adam] sin entered into the world and death through sin, and thus death spread to all men because they had all sinned." (Romans 5:12) Yes, all of us have inherited sin from Adam. Hence, the Bible says that he "sold" himself and his offspring into slavery to sin and death. (Romans 7:14) There was no hope for Adam or Eve because they willfully chose to disobey God. But what about their offspring, including us?

⁷ Jehovah came to mankind's rescue by means of the ransom. What is a ransom? The idea of a ransom basically involves two things. First, a ransom is the price paid to bring about a release or to buy something back. It might be compared to the price

6. **When Adam disobeyed God, what did he lose, and how were his offspring affected?**
7, 8. **A ransom basically involves what two things?**

*What Does the Bible Really Teach?*

paid for the release of a prisoner of war. Second, a ransom is the price that covers, or pays, the cost of something. It is similar to the price paid to cover the damages caused by an injury. For example, if a person causes an accident, he would have to pay an amount that fully corresponds to, or equals, the value of what was damaged.

⁸ How would it be possible to cover the enormous loss that Adam inflicted on all of us and to release us from slavery to sin and death? Let us consider the ransom that Jehovah provided and what this can mean for you.

## HOW JEHOVAH PROVIDED THE RANSOM

⁹ Since a perfect human life was lost, no imperfect human life could ever buy it back. (Psalm 49: 7, 8) What was needed was a ransom equal in value to what was lost. This is in harmony with the principle of perfect justice found in God's Word, which says: "Soul will be for soul." (Deuteronomy 19:21) So, what would cover the value of the perfect human soul, or life, that Adam lost? Another

9. **What sort of ransom was required?**

perfect human life was the "corresponding ransom" that was required.—1 Timothy 2:6.

¹⁰ How did Jehovah provide the ransom? He sent one of his perfect spirit sons to the earth. But Jehovah did not send just any spirit creature. He sent the one most precious to him, his only-begotten Son. (1 John 4:9, 10) Willingly, this Son left his heavenly home. (Philippians 2:7) As we learned in the preceding chapter of this book, Jehovah performed a miracle when he transferred the life of this Son to the womb of Mary. By means of God's holy spirit, Jesus was born as a perfect human and was not under the penalty of sin.—Luke 1:35.

¹¹ How could one man serve as a ransom for many, in fact, millions of humans? Well, how did humans numbering into the millions come to be sinners in the first place? Recall that by sinning, Adam lost the precious possession of perfect human life. Hence, he could not pass it on to his offspring. Instead, he could pass on only sin and death. Jesus, whom the Bible calls "the last Adam,"

10. How did Jehovah provide the ransom?
11. How could one man serve as a ransom for millions?

*What Does the Bible Really Teach?*

had a perfect human life, and he never sinned. (1 Corinthians 15:45) In a sense, Jesus stepped into Adam's place in order to save us. By sacrificing, or giving up, his perfect life in flawless obedience to God, Jesus paid the price for Adam's sin. Jesus thus brought hope to Adam's offspring.—Romans 5:19; 1 Corinthians 15:21, 22.

¹² The Bible describes in detail the suffering that Jesus endured before his death. He experienced harsh whipping, cruel impalement, and an agonizing death on a torture stake. (John 19:1, 16-18, 30; Appendix, pages 261-3) Why was it necessary for Jesus to suffer so much? In a later chapter of this book, we will see that Satan has questioned whether Jehovah has any human servants who would remain faithful under trial. By enduring faithfully in spite of great suffering, Jesus gave the best possible answer to Satan's challenge. Jesus proved that a perfect man possessing free will could keep perfect integrity to God no matter what the Devil did. Jehovah must have rejoiced greatly over the faithfulness of his dear Son!—Proverbs 27:11.

12. What was proved by Jesus' suffering?

**13** How was the ransom paid? On the 14th day of the Jewish month Nisan in 33 C.E., God allowed his perfect and sinless Son to be executed. Jesus thus sacrificed his perfect human life "once for all time." (Hebrews 10:10) On the third day after Jesus died, Jehovah raised him back to spirit life. In heaven, Jesus presented to God the value of his perfect human life sacrificed as a ransom in exchange for Adam's offspring. (Hebrews 9:24) Jehovah accepted the value of Jesus' sacrifice as the ransom needed to deliver mankind from slavery to sin and death. —Romans 3:23, 24.

## WHAT THE RANSOM CAN MEAN FOR YOU

**14** Despite our sinful condition, we can enjoy priceless blessings because of the ransom. Let us consider some of the present and future benefits of this greatest gift from God.

**15** *The forgiveness of sins.* Because of inherited imperfection, we have a real struggle to do what is right. All of us sin either in word or in deed. But

13. How was the ransom paid?
14, 15. To receive "the forgiveness of our sins," what must we do?

*What Does the Bible Really Teach?*

by means of Jesus' ransom sacrifice, we can receive "the forgiveness of our sins." (Colossians 1:13, 14) To gain that forgiveness, however, we must be truly repentant. We must also humbly appeal to Jehovah, asking his forgiveness on the basis of our faith in the ransom sacrifice of his Son.—1 John 1:8, 9.

¹⁶ *A clean conscience before God.* A guilty conscience can easily lead to hopelessness and make us feel worthless. Through the forgiveness made possible by the ransom, though, Jehovah kindly enables us to worship him with a clean conscience despite our imperfection. (Hebrews 9:13, 14) This makes it possible for us to have freeness of speech with Jehovah. Therefore, we can freely approach him in prayer. (Hebrews 4:14-16) Maintaining a clean conscience gives peace of mind, promotes self-respect, and contributes to happiness.

¹⁷ *The hope of everlasting life on a paradise earth.* "The wages sin pays is death," says Romans 6:23. The same verse adds: "But the gift God gives is

16. **What enables us to worship God with a clean conscience, and what is the value of such a conscience?**
17. **What blessings are made possible because Jesus died for us?**

*The Ransom—God's Greatest Gift*

everlasting life by Christ Jesus our Lord." In Chapter 3 of this book, we discussed the blessings of the coming earthly Paradise. (Revelation 21:3, 4) All those future blessings, including life everlasting in perfect health, are made possible because Jesus died for us. To receive those blessings, we need to show that we appreciate the gift of the ransom.

## HOW CAN YOU SHOW YOUR APPRECIATION?

18 Why should we be deeply grateful to Jehovah for the ransom? Well, a gift is especially precious when it involves a sacrifice of time, effort, or expense on the part of the giver. Our heart is touched when we see that a gift is an expression of the giver's genuine love for us. The ransom is the most precious of all gifts, for God made the greatest sacrifice ever in providing it. "God loved the world so much that he gave his only-begotten Son," says John 3:16. The ransom is the most outstanding evidence of Jehovah's love for us. It is also proof of Jesus' love, for he willingly gave his life in our behalf.

18. Why should we be grateful to Jehovah for the provision of the ransom?

(John 15:13) The gift of the ransom should therefore convince us that Jehovah and his Son love us as individuals.—Galatians 2:20.

[19] How, then, can you demonstrate that you appreciate God's gift of the ransom? To begin with, *get to know more about the Great Giver, Jehovah.* (John 17:3) A study of the Bible with the aid of this publication will help you to do that. As you grow in knowledge of Jehovah, your love for him will deepen. In turn, that love will make you want to please him.—1 John 5:3.

[20] *Exercise faith in Jesus' ransom sacrifice.* Jesus himself said: "He that exercises faith in the Son has everlasting life." (John 3:36) How can we exercise faith in Jesus? Such faith is not shown by words alone. "Faith without works is dead," says James 2:26. Yes, true faith is proved by "works," that is, by our actions. One way to show that we have faith in Jesus is by doing our best to imitate him not just in what we say but also in what we do.—John 13:15.

**19, 20. In what ways can you show that you appreciate God's gift of the ransom?**

²¹ *Attend the annual observance of the Lord's Evening Meal.* On the evening of Nisan 14, 33 C.E., Jesus introduced a special observance that the Bible calls "the Lord's evening meal." (1 Corinthians 11:20; Matthew 26:26-28) This observance is also called the Memorial of Christ's death. Jesus instituted it to help his apostles and all true Christians after them to bear in mind that by means of his death as a perfect human, he gave his soul, or life, as a ransom. Regarding this observance, Jesus commanded: "Keep doing this in remembrance of me." (Luke 22: 19) Observing the Memorial reminds us of the great love shown by both Jehovah and Jesus in connection with the ransom. We can show our appreciation for the ransom by being present at the yearly observance of the Memorial of Jesus' death.*

²² Jehovah's provision of the ransom is indeed an invaluable gift. (2 Corinthians 9:14, 15) This priceless gift can benefit even those who have died. Chapters 6 and 7 will explain how.

---

* For more information about the meaning of the Lord's Evening Meal, see the Appendix, pages 263-6.

**21, 22. (a) Why should we attend the annual observance of the Lord's Evening Meal? (b) What will be explained in Chapters 6 and 7?**

*What Does the Bible Really Teach?*

# WHAT THE BIBLE TEACHES

- The ransom is Jehovah's means to deliver humankind from sin and death.—Ephesians 1:7.

- Jehovah provided the ransom by sending his only-begotten Son to earth to die for us. —1 John 4:9, 10.

- By means of the ransom, we gain the forgiveness of sins, a clean conscience, and the hope of everlasting life.—1 John 1:8, 9.

- We show that we appreciate the ransom by getting to know more about Jehovah, by exercising faith in Jesus' ransom sacrifice, and by attending the Lord's Evening Meal. —John 3:16.

# CHAPTER SIX

# Where Are the Dead?

## What happens to us when we die?

## Why do we die?

## Would it be comforting to know the truth about death?

THESE are questions that people have thought about for thousands of years. They are important questions. No matter who we are or where we live, the answers concern each one of us.

[2] In the preceding chapter, we discussed how the ransom sacrifice of Jesus Christ opened the way to everlasting life. We also learned that the Bible foretells a time when "death will be no more." (Revelation 21:4) Meanwhile, we all die. "The living are conscious that they will die," said wise King Solomon. (Ecclesiastes 9:5) We try to live as long as possible. Still, we wonder what will happen to us when we die.

1-3. What questions do people ask about death, and what answers do various religions offer?

³ When our loved ones die, we mourn. And we may ask: 'What has happened to them? Are they suffering? Are they watching over us? Can we help them? Will we ever see them again?' The world's religions offer differing answers to these questions. Some teach that if you live a good life, you will go to heaven but if you live a bad life, you will burn in a place of torment. Other religions teach that at death, people pass on to the spirit realm to be with their ancestors. Still other religions teach that the dead go to an underworld to be judged and are then reincarnated, or reborn in another body.

⁴ Such religious teachings all share one basic idea —that some part of us survives the death of the physical body. According to almost every religion, past and present, we somehow live on forever with the ability to see, hear, and think. Yet, how can that be? Our senses, along with our thoughts, are all linked to the workings of our brain. At death, the brain stops working. Our memories, feelings, and senses do not continue to function independently in

**4. What basic idea do many religions share concerning death?**

some mysterious way. They do not survive the destruction of our brain.

## WHAT REALLY HAPPENS AT DEATH?

5 What happens at death is no mystery to Jehovah, the Creator of the brain. He knows the truth, and in his Word, the Bible, he explains the condition of the dead. Its clear teaching is this: *When a person dies, he ceases to exist.* Death is the opposite of life. The dead do not see or hear or think. Not even one part of us survives the death of the body. We do not possess an immortal soul or spirit.*

6 After Solomon observed that the living know that they will die, he wrote: "As for the dead, they are conscious of *nothing at all.*" He then enlarged on that basic truth by saying that the dead can neither love nor hate and that "there is no work nor devising nor knowledge nor wisdom in [the grave]." (Ecclesiastes 9:5, 6, 10) Similarly, Psalm 146:4 says that when a man dies, "his thoughts do perish." We are mortal and do not survive the death of our

* For a discussion of the words "soul" and "spirit," please see the Appendix, pages 266-71.

**5, 6. What does the Bible teach about the condition of the dead?**

body. The life we enjoy is like the flame of a candle. When the flame is put out, it does not *go* anywhere. It is simply gone.

## WHAT JESUS SAID ABOUT DEATH

[7] Jesus Christ spoke about the condition of the dead. He did so with regard to Lazarus, a man whom he knew well and who had died. Jesus told his disciples: "Lazarus our friend has gone to rest." The disciples thought that Jesus meant that Lazarus was resting in sleep, recovering from an illness. They were wrong. Jesus explained: "Lazarus has died." (John 11:11-14) Notice that Jesus compared death to rest and sleep. Lazarus was neither in heaven nor in a burning hell. He was not meeting angels or ancestors. Lazarus was not being reborn as another human. He was at rest in death, as though in a deep sleep without dreams. Other scriptures also compare death to sleep. For example, when the disciple Stephen was stoned to death, the Bible says that he "fell asleep." (Acts 7:60) Similarly, the apostle Paul wrote about some in his day who had "fallen asleep" in death.—1 Corinthians 15:6.

**7. How did Jesus explain what death is like?**

*Where Are the Dead?*                                                     73

**8** Was it God's original purpose for people to die? Not at all! Jehovah made man to live forever on earth. As we learned earlier in this book, God placed the first human couple in a delightful paradise. He blessed them with perfect health. Jehovah wanted only good for them. Does any loving parent want his children to suffer the pain of old age and death? Of course not! Jehovah loved his children and wanted them to enjoy endless happiness on earth. Concerning humans, the Bible says: "Time indefinite [Jehovah] has put in their heart." (Ecclesiastes 3:11) God created us with the desire to live forever. And he has opened the way for that desire to be fulfilled.

## WHY HUMANS DIE

**9** Why, then, do humans die? To find the answer, we must consider what happened when there was only one man and one woman on earth. The Bible explains: "Jehovah God made to grow out of the ground every tree desirable to one's sight and good

---

8. How do we know that it was not God's purpose for people to die?
9. What restriction did Jehovah place upon Adam, and why was this command not difficult to obey?

*What Does the Bible Really Teach?*

for food." (Genesis 2:9) However, there was one restriction. Jehovah told Adam: "From every tree of the garden you may eat to satisfaction. But as for the tree of the knowledge of good and bad you must not eat from it, for in the day you eat from it you will positively die." (Genesis 2:16, 17) This command was not difficult to obey. There were many other trees from which Adam and Eve could eat. But they now received a special opportunity to show their gratitude to the One who had given them everything, including perfect life. Their obedience would also show that they respected the authority of their heavenly Father and that they wanted his loving direction.

10 Sadly, the first human couple chose to disobey Jehovah. Speaking through a serpent, Satan asked Eve: "Is it really so that God said you must not eat from every tree of the garden?" Eve replied: "Of the fruit of the trees of the garden we may eat. But as for eating of the fruit of the tree that is in the

10, 11. (a) How did the first human couple come to disobey God? (b) Why was the disobedience of Adam and Eve a serious matter?

middle of the garden, God has said, 'You must not eat from it, no, you must not touch it that you do not die.'"—Genesis 3:1-3.

[11] "You positively will not die," said Satan. "God knows that in the very day of your eating from it your eyes are bound to be opened and you are bound to be like God, knowing good and bad." (Genesis 3:4, 5) Satan wanted Eve to believe that she would benefit by eating the forbidden fruit. According to him, she could decide for herself what was right and what was wrong; she could do what she wanted. Satan also charged that Jehovah had lied about the consequences of eating the fruit. Eve believed Satan. So she picked some of the fruit and ate it. She then gave some to her husband, and he too ate some of it. They did not act in ignorance. They knew that they were doing exactly what God had told them *not* to do. By eating the fruit, they deliberately disobeyed a simple and reasonable command. They showed contempt for their heavenly Father and his authority. Such disrespect for their loving Creator was inexcusable!

*What Does the Bible Really Teach?*

¹² To illustrate: How would you feel if you raised and cared for a son or a daughter who then disobeyed you in a way that showed that he or she had no respect or love for you? That would cause you much heartache. Imagine, then, how hurt Jehovah must have felt when both Adam and Eve took a course of opposition to him.

¹³ Jehovah had no reason to sustain disobedient Adam and Eve forever. They died, just as he had said they would. Adam and Eve ceased to exist. They did not pass on to the spirit realm. We know this because of what Jehovah said to Adam after confronting him with his disobedience. God said: "You [will] return to the ground, for out of it you were taken. For dust you are and to dust you will return." (Genesis 3:19) God had made Adam from the dust of the ground. (Genesis 2:7) Before that, Adam did not exist. Therefore, when Jehovah said that Adam would return to the dust, He meant that

**12.** What may help us to understand how Jehovah felt when Adam and Eve took a course of opposition to him?

**13.** What did Jehovah say would happen to Adam at death, and what does this mean?

Adam would return to a state of nonexistence. Adam would be as lifeless as the dust from which he was made.

14 Adam and Eve could have been alive today, but they died because they chose to disobey God and thus sinned. The reason we die is that Adam's sinful condition as well as death was passed on to all of his descendants. (Romans 5:12) That sin is like a terrible inherited disease from which no one can escape. Its consequence, death, is a curse. Death is an enemy, not a friend. (1 Corinthians 15:26) How grateful we can be that Jehovah provided the ransom to rescue us from this dreadful enemy!

## KNOWING THE TRUTH ABOUT DEATH IS BENEFICIAL

15 What the Bible teaches about the condition of the dead is comforting. As we have seen, the dead do not suffer pain or heartache. There is no reason to be afraid of them, for they cannot harm us. They do not need our help, and they cannot help us. We cannot speak with them, and they cannot speak

14. Why do we die?
15. Why is it comforting to know the truth about death?

*What Does the Bible Really Teach?*

with us. Many religious leaders falsely claim that they can help those who have died, and people who believe such leaders give them money. But knowing the truth protects us from being deceived by those who teach such lies.

¹⁶ Does your religion agree with what the Bible teaches about the dead? Most do not. Why? Because their teachings have been influenced by Satan. He uses false religion to get people to believe that after their body dies, they will continue to live in the spirit realm. This is a lie that Satan combines with other lies to turn people away from Jehovah God. How so?

¹⁷ As noted earlier, some religions teach that if a person lives a bad life, after death he will go to a place of fiery torment to suffer forever. This teaching dishonors God. Jehovah is a God of love and would never make people suffer in this way. (1 John 4:8) How would you feel about a man who punished a disobedient child by holding his hands in a fire?

16. **Who has influenced the teachings of many religions, and in what way?**
17. **Why does the teaching of eternal torment dishonor Jehovah?**

Would you respect such a man? In fact, would you even want to get to know him? Definitely not! You would likely think that he was very cruel. Yet, Satan wants us to believe that Jehovah tortures people in fire forever—for countless billions of years!

¹⁸ Satan also uses some religions to teach that after death people become spirits who must be respected and honored by the living. According to this teaching, the spirits of the dead can become powerful friends or terrible enemies. Many people believe this lie. They fear the dead and give them honor and worship. In contrast, the Bible teaches that the dead are sleeping and that we should worship only the true God, Jehovah, our Creator and Provider.—Revelation 4:11.

¹⁹ Knowing the truth about the dead protects you from being misled by religious lies. It also helps you to understand other Bible teachings. For example, when you realize that people do not pass on to the spirit realm at death, the promise of everlasting

**18. Worship of the dead is based on what religious lie?**
**19. Knowing the truth about death helps us to understand what other Bible teaching?**

life on a paradise earth takes on real meaning for you.

**20** Long ago, the righteous man Job raised this question: "If an able-bodied man dies can he live again?" (Job 14:14) Can a lifeless person who is sleeping in death be brought back to life? What the Bible teaches about this is deeply comforting, as the next chapter will show.

**20. What question will we consider in the next chapter?**

---

## WHAT THE BIBLE TEACHES

- The dead do not see or hear or think.
  —Ecclesiastes 9:5.

- The dead are at rest; they do not suffer.
  —John 11:11.

- We die because we inherited sin from Adam.
  —Romans 5:12.

---

# CHAPTER SEVEN

# Real Hope for Your Loved Ones Who Have Died

### How do we know that the resurrection will really happen?

### How does Jehovah feel about resurrecting the dead?

### Who will be resurrected?

IMAGINE that you are running away from a vicious enemy. He is much stronger and faster than you are. You know that he is merciless because you have seen him kill some of your friends. No matter how hard you try to outrun him, he keeps getting closer. There seems to be no hope. Suddenly, though, a rescuer appears at your side. He is far more powerful than your enemy, and he promises to help you. How relieved that makes you feel!

² In a sense, you *are* being pursued by such an enemy. All of us are. As we learned in the preceding

1-3. **What enemy pursues all of us, and why will considering what the Bible teaches bring us some relief?**

*What Does the Bible Really Teach?*

chapter, the Bible calls death an enemy. None of us can outrun it or fight it off. Most of us have seen this enemy claim the lives of people dear to us. But Jehovah is far more powerful than death. He is the loving Rescuer who has already shown that he can defeat this enemy. And he promises to destroy this enemy, death, once and for all. The Bible teaches: "As the last enemy, death is to be brought to nothing." (1 Corinthians 15:26) That is good news!

³ Let us take a brief look at how the enemy death affects us when it strikes. Doing this will help us to appreciate something that will make us happy. You see, Jehovah promises that the dead will live again. (Isaiah 26:19) They will be brought back to life. That is the hope of the resurrection.

## WHEN A LOVED ONE DIES

⁴ Have you lost a loved one in death? The pain, the grief, and the feelings of helplessness can seem unbearable. At such times, we need to go to God's Word for comfort. (2 Corinthians 1:3, 4) The Bible

---

**4. (a)** Why does Jesus' reaction to the death of a loved one teach us about Jehovah's feelings? **(b)** Jesus developed what special friendship?

helps us to understand how Jehovah and Jesus feel about death. Jesus, who perfectly reflected his Father, knew the pain of losing someone in death. (John 14:9) When he was in Jerusalem, Jesus used to visit Lazarus and his sisters, Mary and Martha, who lived in the nearby town of Bethany. They became close friends. The Bible says: "Jesus loved Martha and her sister and Lazarus." (John 11:5) As we learned in the preceding chapter, though, Lazarus died.

⁵ How did Jesus feel about losing his friend? The account tells us that Jesus joined Lazarus' relatives and friends as they grieved over this loss. Seeing them, Jesus was deeply moved. He "groaned in the spirit and became troubled." Then, the account says, "Jesus gave way to tears." (John 11:33, 35) Did Jesus' grief mean that he had no hope? Not at all. In fact, Jesus knew that something wonderful was about to happen. (John 11:3, 4) Still, he felt the pain and sorrow that death brings.

5, 6. (a) How did Jesus respond when he was with Lazarus' grieving family and friends? (b) Why is Jesus' grief encouraging to us?

*What Does the Bible Really Teach?*

**6** In a way, Jesus' grief is encouraging to us. It teaches us that Jesus and his Father, Jehovah, hate death. But Jehovah God is able to fight and overcome that enemy! Let us see what God enabled Jesus to do.

## "LAZARUS, COME ON OUT!"

**7** Lazarus had been buried in a cave, and Jesus asked that the stone sealing its entrance be taken away. Martha objected because after four days, Lazarus' body must have begun to decay. (John 11:39) From a human standpoint, what hope was there?

**8** The stone was rolled away, and Jesus cried out with a loud voice: "Lazarus, come on out!" What happened? "The man that had been dead came out." (John 11:43, 44) Can you imagine the joy of the people there? Whether Lazarus was their brother, relative, friend, or neighbor, they knew that he had died. Yet, here he was—the same dear man—standing among them again. That must have seemed too good to be true. Many no doubt embraced Lazarus joyfully. What a victory over death!

**7, 8. Why might the case of Lazarus have seemed hopeless to human onlookers, but what did Jesus do?**

⁹ Jesus did not claim to perform this amazing miracle on his own. In his prayer just before calling out to Lazarus, he made it clear that Jehovah was the Source of the resurrection. (John 11:41, 42) This was not the only time that Jehovah used his power in this way. The resurrection of Lazarus is just one of nine miracles of this kind recorded in God's Word.* To read and study these accounts is a delight. They teach us that God is not partial, for the resurrected ones include young and old, male and female, Israelite and non-Israelite. And what joy is described in these passages! For example, when Jesus raised a young girl from the dead, her parents "were beside themselves with great ecstasy." (Mark 5:42) Yes, Jehovah had given them a cause for joy that they would never forget.

¹⁰ Of course, those resurrected by Jesus eventually died again. Does this mean that it was pointless

---

* The other accounts are found at 1 Kings 17:17-24; 2 Kings 4:32-37; 13:20, 21; Matthew 28:5-7; Luke 7:11-17; 8:40-56; Acts 9:36-42; and 20:7-12.

**9, 10. (a) How did Jesus reveal the Source of his power to resurrect Lazarus? (b) What are some of the benefits of reading the Bible's resurrection accounts?**

*What Does the Bible Really Teach?*

to resurrect them? Not at all. These Bible accounts confirm important truths and give us hope.

## LEARNING FROM THE RESURRECTION ACCOUNTS

11 The Bible teaches that the dead "are conscious of nothing at all." They are not alive and have no conscious existence anywhere. The account of Lazarus confirms this. Upon returning to life, did Lazarus thrill people with descriptions of heaven? Or did he terrify them with horrible tales about a burning hell? No. The Bible contains no such words from Lazarus. During the four days that he was dead, he had been "conscious of nothing at all." (Ecclesiastes 9:5) Lazarus had simply been sleeping in death.—John 11:11.

12 The account of Lazarus also teaches us that the resurrection is a reality, not a mere myth. Jesus raised Lazarus in front of a crowd of eyewitnesses. Even the religious leaders, who hated Jesus, did not

11. How does the account of Lazarus' resurrection help to confirm the truth recorded at Ecclesiastes 9:5?

12. Why can we be sure that the resurrection of Lazarus really happened?

deny this miracle. Rather, they said: "What are we to do, because this man [Jesus] performs many signs?" (John 11:47) Many people went to see the resurrected man. As a result, even more of them put faith in Jesus. They saw in Lazarus living proof that Jesus was sent by God. This evidence was so powerful that some of the hardhearted Jewish religious leaders planned to kill both Jesus and Lazarus.—John 11:53; 12:9-11.

13 Is it unrealistic to accept the resurrection as a fact? No, for Jesus taught that someday "all those in the memorial tombs" will be resurrected. (John 5:28) Jehovah is the Creator of all life. Should it be hard to believe that he can re-create life? Of course, much would depend on Jehovah's memory. Can he remember our dead loved ones? Countless trillions of stars fill the universe, yet God gives the name of each one! (Isaiah 40:26) So Jehovah God can remember our dead loved ones in every detail, and he is ready to restore them to life.

13. **What basis do we have for believing that Jehovah really can resurrect the dead?**

**14** How, though, does Jehovah feel about resurrecting the dead? The Bible teaches that he is eager to raise the dead. The faithful man Job asked: "If an able-bodied man dies can he live again?" Job was speaking about waiting in the grave until the time came for God to remember him. He said to Jehovah: "You will call, and I myself shall answer you. For the work of your hands you will have a yearning."—Job 14:13-15.

**15** Just think! Jehovah actually yearns to bring the dead back to life. Is it not heartwarming to learn that Jehovah feels that way? But what about this future resurrection? Who will be resurrected, and where?

## "ALL THOSE IN THE MEMORIAL TOMBS"

**16** The Bible's resurrection accounts teach us much about the resurrection to come. People who were restored to life right here on earth were reunited with their loved ones. The future resurrection will be similar—but much better. As we learned in

---

**14, 15.** As illustrated by what Job said, how does Jehovah feel about bringing the dead back to life?

**16.** The dead will be resurrected to live in what kind of conditions?

Chapter 3, God's purpose is that the whole earth be made into a paradise. So the dead will not be raised to life in a world filled with war, crime, and sickness. They will have an opportunity to live forever on this earth in peaceful and happy conditions.

<sup></sup>17 Who will be resurrected? Jesus said that *"all those in the memorial tombs will hear his [Jesus'] voice and come out."* (John 5:28, 29) Similarly, Revelation 20:13 says: "The sea gave up those dead in it, and death and Hades gave up those dead in them." "Hades" refers to the common grave of mankind. (See the Appendix, pages 271-3.) This collective grave will be emptied. All those billions who rest there will live again. The apostle Paul said: "There is going to be a resurrection of both the righteous and the unrighteous." (Acts 24:15) What does that mean?

18 "The righteous" include many of the people we read about in the Bible who lived before Jesus came to the earth. You might think of Noah, Abraham,

17. How extensive will the resurrection be?
18. Who are included among "the righteous" who are to be resurrected, and how may this hope affect you personally?

*What Does the Bible Really Teach?*

Sarah, Moses, Ruth, Esther, and many others. Some of these men and women of faith are discussed in the 11th chapter of Hebrews. But "the righteous" also include Jehovah's servants who die in our time. Thanks to the resurrection hope, we may be freed from any dread of dying.—Hebrews 2:15.

[19] What about all the people who did not serve or obey Jehovah because they never knew about him? These billions of "unrighteous" ones will not be forgotten. They too will be resurrected and given time to learn about the true God and to serve him. During a period of a thousand years, the dead will be resurrected and given an opportunity to join faithful humans on earth in serving Jehovah. It will be a wonderful time. This period is what the Bible refers to as Judgment Day.*

[20] Does this mean that every human who ever lived will be resurrected? No. The Bible says that some of the dead are in "Gehenna." (Luke 12:5)

---

* For more information on Judgment Day and the basis for judgment, please see the Appendix, pages 273-6.

---

**19. Who are "the unrighteous," and what opportunity does Jehovah kindly give them?**
**20. What is Gehenna, and who go there?**

Gehenna got its name from a garbage dump located outside of ancient Jerusalem. Dead bodies and garbage were burned there. The dead whose bodies were thrown there were considered by the Jews to be unworthy of a burial and a resurrection. So Gehenna is a fitting symbol of everlasting destruction. Although Jesus will have a role in judging the living and the dead, Jehovah is the final Judge. (Acts 10:42) He will never resurrect those whom he judges to be wicked and unwilling to change.

## THE HEAVENLY RESURRECTION

21 The Bible also refers to another kind of resurrection, one to life as a spirit creature in heaven. Only one example of this type of resurrection is recorded in the Bible, that of Jesus Christ.

22 After Jesus was put to death as a human, Jehovah did not allow His faithful Son to remain in the grave. (Psalm 16:10; Acts 13:34, 35) God resurrected Jesus, but not as a human. The apostle Peter explains that Christ was "put to death in the flesh, but . . . made alive in the spirit." (1 Peter 3:18) This tru-

21, 22. (a) What other kind of resurrection is there? (b) Who was the first ever to receive a resurrection to spirit life?

ly was a great miracle. Jesus was alive again as a mighty spirit person! (1 Corinthians 15:3-6) Jesus was the first ever to receive this glorious type of resurrection. (John 3:13) But he would not be the last.

23 Knowing that he would soon return to heaven, Jesus told his faithful followers that he would "prepare a place" for them there. (John 14:2) Jesus referred to those going to heaven as his "little flock." (Luke 12:32) How many are to be in this relatively small group of faithful Christians? According to Revelation 14:1, the apostle John says: "I saw, and, look! the Lamb [Jesus Christ] standing upon the Mount Zion, and with him a hundred and forty-four thousand having his name and the name of his Father written on their foreheads."

24 These 144,000 Christians, including Jesus' faithful apostles, are raised to life in heaven. When does their resurrection take place? The apostle Paul wrote that it would occur during the time of Christ's presence. (1 Corinthians 15:23) As you will learn in Chapter 9, we are now living in that time.

23, 24. Who make up Jesus' "little flock," and how many will they number?

So those few remaining ones of the 144,000 who die in our day are instantly resurrected to life in heaven. (1 Corinthians 15:51-55) The vast majority of mankind, however, have the prospect of being resurrected in the future to life in Paradise on earth.

<sup>25</sup> Yes, Jehovah really will defeat our enemy death, and it will be gone forever! (Isaiah 25:8) Yet, you may wonder, 'What will those resurrected to heaven do there?' They will form part of a marvelous Kingdom government in heaven. We will learn more about that government in the next chapter.

**25. What will be considered in the next chapter?**

---

## WHAT THE BIBLE TEACHES

- The Bible's resurrection accounts give us a sure hope.—John 11:39-44.

- Jehovah is eager to bring the dead back to life. —Job 14:13-15.

- All of those in the common grave of mankind will be resurrected.—John 5:28, 29.

# CHAPTER EIGHT

# What Is God's Kingdom?

**What does the Bible tell us about
the Kingdom of God?**

**What will God's Kingdom do?**

**When will the Kingdom cause God's will
to be done on earth?**

MILLIONS of people worldwide are familiar with the prayer that many call the Our Father, or the Lord's Prayer. Both expressions refer to a famous prayer given as a model by Jesus Christ himself. It is a very meaningful prayer, and a consideration of its first three petitions will help you to learn more about what the Bible really teaches.

² At the beginning of this model prayer, Jesus instructed his hearers: "You must pray, then, this way: 'Our Father in the heavens, let your name be sanctified. Let your kingdom come. Let your

1. **What famous prayer will now be examined?**
2. **What were three of the things that Jesus taught his disciples to pray for?**

will take place, as in heaven, also upon earth.'" (Matthew 6:9-13) What is the significance of these three petitions?

³ We have already learned a lot about God's name, Jehovah. And to some extent we have discussed God's will—what he has done and will yet do for mankind. To what, though, was Jesus referring when he told us to pray: "Let your kingdom come"? What is God's Kingdom? How will its coming sanctify God's name, or make it holy? And how is the coming of the Kingdom related to the doing of God's will?

## WHAT GOD'S KINGDOM IS

⁴ God's Kingdom is a government established by Jehovah God with a King chosen by God. Who is the King of God's Kingdom? Jesus Christ. Jesus as King is greater than all human rulers and is called "the King of those who rule as kings and Lord of those who rule as lords." (1 Timothy 6:15) He has the power to do far more good than *any* human ruler, even the best among them.

3. What do we need to know about God's Kingdom?
4. What is God's Kingdom, and who is its King?

*What Does the Bible Really Teach?*

⁵ From where will God's Kingdom rule? Well, where is Jesus? You will remember learning that he was put to death on a torture stake, and then he was resurrected. Shortly thereafter, he ascended to heaven. (Acts 2:33) Hence, that is where God's Kingdom is—in heaven. That is why the Bible calls it a "heavenly kingdom." (2 Timothy 4:18) Although God's Kingdom is in heaven, it will rule over the earth.—Revelation 11:15.

⁶ What makes Jesus an outstanding King? For one thing, he will never die. Comparing Jesus with human kings, the Bible calls him "the one alone having immortality, who dwells in unapproachable light." (1 Timothy 6:16) This means that all the good that Jesus does will last. And he *will* do great and good things.

⁷ Consider this Bible prophecy about Jesus: "Upon him the spirit of Jehovah must settle down, the spirit of wisdom and of understanding, the spirit of counsel and of mightiness, the spirit of

5. From where does God's Kingdom rule, and over what?
6, 7. What makes Jesus an outstanding King?

knowledge and of the fear of Jehovah; and there will be enjoyment by him in the fear of Jehovah. And he will not judge by any mere appearance to his eyes, nor reprove simply according to the thing heard by his ears. And with righteousness he must judge the lowly ones, and with uprightness he must give reproof in behalf of the meek ones of the earth." (Isaiah 11:2-4) Those words show that Jesus was to be a righteous and compassionate King over people on earth. Would you want to have a ruler like that?

⁸ Here is another truth about God's Kingdom: Jesus will not rule alone. He will have corulers. For example, the apostle Paul told Timothy: "If we go on enduring, we shall also rule together as kings." (2 Timothy 2:12) Yes, Paul, Timothy, and other faithful ones who have been selected by God will rule together with Jesus in the heavenly Kingdom. How many will have that privilege?

⁹ As pointed out in Chapter 7 of this book,

**8. Who will rule with Jesus?**
**9. How many will rule with Jesus, and when did God start to choose them?**

*What Does the Bible Really Teach?*

the apostle John was given a vision in which he saw "the Lamb [Jesus Christ] standing upon the Mount Zion [his royal position in heaven], and with him a hundred and forty-four thousand having his name and the name of his Father written on their foreheads." Who are those 144,000? John himself tells us: "These are the ones that keep following the Lamb no matter where he goes. These were bought from among mankind as firstfruits to God and to the Lamb." (Revelation 14:1, 4) Yes, they are faithful followers of Jesus Christ specially chosen to rule in heaven with him. After being raised out of death to heavenly life, "they are to rule as kings over the earth" along with Jesus. (Revelation 5:10) Since the days of the apostles, God has been selecting faithful Christians in order to complete the number 144,000.

10 To arrange for Jesus and the 144,000 to rule mankind is very loving. For one thing, Jesus knows what it is like to be a human and to suffer. Paul

10. Why is it a loving arrangement for Jesus and the 144,000 to rule over mankind?

*What Is God's Kingdom?*

said that Jesus is "not one who cannot sympathize with our weaknesses, but one who has been tested in all respects like ourselves, but without sin." (Hebrews 4:15; 5:8) His corulers too have suffered and endured as humans. In addition, they have struggled with imperfection and coped with all kinds of sickness. Surely, they will understand the problems that humans face!

## WHAT WILL GOD'S KINGDOM DO?

11 When Jesus said that his disciples should pray for God's Kingdom to come, he also said that they should pray for God's will to be done "as in heaven, also upon earth." God is in heaven, and his will has always been done there by the faithful angels. In Chapter 3 of this book, however, we learned that a wicked angel stopped doing God's will and caused Adam and Eve to sin. In Chapter 10, we will learn more about what the Bible teaches regarding that wicked angel, whom we know as Satan the Devil. Satan and the an-

**11. Why did Jesus say that his disciples should pray for God's will to be done in heaven?**

*What Does the Bible Really Teach?*

gelic spirit creatures who chose to follow him —called demons—were allowed to stay in heaven for a while. Hence, not all in heaven were then doing God's will. That was to change when God's Kingdom would begin to rule. The newly enthroned King, Jesus Christ, was to wage war on Satan.—Revelation 12:7-9.

¹² The following prophetic words describe what would happen: "I heard a loud voice in heaven say: 'Now have come to pass the salvation and the power and the kingdom of our God and the authority of his Christ, because the accuser of our brothers [Satan] has been hurled down, who accuses them day and night before our God!'" (Revelation 12:10) Did you notice two very important events described in that Bible verse? First, God's Kingdom under Jesus Christ begins to rule. Second, Satan is cast out of heaven down to the earth.

¹³ What have been the results of those two events? Regarding what happened in heaven, we

12. What two important events are described at Revelation 12:10?
13. What has been the result of Satan's being cast out of heaven?

read: "On this account be glad, you heavens and you who reside in them!" (Revelation 12:12) Yes, the faithful angels in heaven rejoice because, with Satan and his demons gone, everyone in heaven is faithful to Jehovah God. There is complete, unbroken peace and harmony there. God's will is being done in heaven.

14 What, though, about the earth? The Bible says: "Woe for the earth and for the sea, because the Devil has come down to you, having great anger, knowing he has a short period of time." (Revelation 12:12) Satan is angry about being cast out of heaven and having just a short time left. In his anger he causes distress, or "woe," on earth. We will learn more about that "woe" in the next chapter. But with that in mind, we could ask, How can the Kingdom cause God's will to be done on earth?

15 Well, remember what God's will is for the earth. You learned about it in Chapter 3. In Eden,

14. What has happened because Satan has been cast down to the earth?
15. What is God's will for the earth?

*What Does the Bible Really Teach?*

God showed that his will is for this earth to be a paradise filled with an undying, righteous human race. Satan caused Adam and Eve to sin, and that affected the fulfillment of God's will for the earth but did not change it. Jehovah still purposes that "the righteous themselves will possess the earth, and they will reside forever upon it." (Psalm 37:29) And God's Kingdom will accomplish that. In what way?

¹⁶ Consider the prophecy found at Daniel 2:44. There we read: "In the days of those kings the God of heaven will set up a kingdom that will never be brought to ruin. And the kingdom itself will not be passed on to any other people. It will crush and put an end to all these kingdoms, and it itself will stand to times indefinite." What does this tell us about God's Kingdom?

¹⁷ First, it tells us that God's Kingdom was to be established "in the days of those kings," or while other kingdoms still existed. Second, it tells us that the Kingdom will last forever. It will not be

**16, 17. What does Daniel 2:44 tell us about God's Kingdom?**

*What Is God's Kingdom?*

conquered and be replaced by some other government. Third, we see that there will be war between God's Kingdom and the kingdoms of this world. God's Kingdom will be victorious. In the end, it will be the only government over mankind. Then humans will enjoy the best rulership they have ever known.

18 The Bible has much to say about that final war between God's Kingdom and the governments of this world. For example, it teaches that as the end approaches, wicked spirits will spread lies to deceive "the kings of the entire inhabited earth." For what purpose? "To gather them [the kings] together to the war of the great day of God the Almighty." The kings of the earth will be gathered together to "the place that is called in Hebrew Har–Magedon." (Revelation 16:14, 16) Because of what is said in those two verses, the final conflict between human governments and God's Kingdom is called the battle of Har–Magedon, or Armageddon.

**18. What is the name of the final war between God's Kingdom and the governments of this world?**

*What Does the Bible Really Teach?*

19 What will God's Kingdom achieve by means of Armageddon? Think again about what God's will is for the earth. Jehovah God purposed that the earth be filled with a righteous, perfect human race serving him in Paradise. What prevents that from happening right now? First, we are sinful, and we get sick and die. We learned in Chapter 5, however, that Jesus died for us so that we can live forever. Likely you remember the words recorded in the Gospel of John: "God loved the world so much that he gave his only-begotten Son, in order that everyone exercising faith in him might not be destroyed but have everlasting life."—John 3:16.

20 Another problem is that many people do wicked things. They lie, cheat, and commit immorality. They do not *want* to do God's will. People who do wicked things will be destroyed during God's war of Armageddon. (Psalm 37:10) Yet another reason why God's will is not being done on earth is that governments do not encourage people to do it. Many governments have been weak, cruel, or

19, 20. **What prevents God's will from being done on earth right now?**

*What Is God's Kingdom?*

corrupt. The Bible frankly says: "Man has dominated man to his injury."—Ecclesiastes 8:9.

21 After Armageddon, mankind will be under just one government, God's Kingdom. That Kingdom will do God's will and bring wonderful blessings. For example, it will remove Satan and his demons. (Revelation 20:1-3) The power of Jesus' sacrifice will be applied so that faithful humans will no longer get sick and die. Instead, under Kingdom rule they will be able to live forever. (Revelation 22:1-3) The earth will be made into a paradise. Thus the Kingdom will cause God's will to be done on earth and will sanctify God's name. What does this mean? It means that eventually under God's Kingdom everyone alive will honor Jehovah's name.

## WHEN DOES GOD'S KINGDOM ACT?

22 When Jesus told his followers to pray, "Let your kingdom come," it was clear that the Kingdom had not come at that time. Did it come when

21. How will the Kingdom cause God's will to be done on earth?
22. Why do we know that God's Kingdom did not come when Jesus was on earth or immediately after he was resurrected?

*What Does the Bible Really Teach?*

Jesus ascended to heaven? No, because both Peter and Paul said that after Jesus was resurrected, the prophecy at Psalm 110:1 was fulfilled in him: "The utterance of Jehovah to my Lord is: 'Sit at my right hand until I place your enemies as a stool for your feet.'" (Acts 2:32-34; Hebrews 10:12, 13) There was a waiting period.

23 For how long? During the 19th century, sincere Bible students calculated that the waiting period would end in 1914. (Regarding this date, see the Appendix, pages 276-9.) World events that began in 1914 confirm that the calculation of these sincere Bible students was correct. The fulfillment of Bible prophecy shows that in 1914, Christ became King and God's heavenly Kingdom began to rule. Hence, we are living in the "short period of time" that Satan has left. (Revelation 12:12; Psalm 110:2) We can also say with certainty that soon God's Kingdom will act to cause God's will to be done on earth. Do you find this to be wonderful

23. (a) When did God's Kingdom begin to rule? (b) What will be discussed in the next chapter?

news? Do you believe that it is true? The next chapter will help you to see that the Bible really does teach these things.

---

### WHAT THE BIBLE TEACHES

- God's Kingdom is a heavenly government with Jesus Christ as King, and from among mankind, 144,000 are taken to rule with him. —Revelation 14:1, 4.

- The Kingdom started to rule in 1914, and since then Satan has been cast out of heaven down to earth.—Revelation 12:9.

- God's Kingdom will soon destroy human governments, and the earth will become a paradise.—Revelation 16:14, 16.

---

*What Does the Bible Really Teach?*

# CHAPTER NINE

# Are We Living in "the Last Days"?

**What events in our time were foretold in the Bible?**

**What does God's Word say people would be like in "the last days"?**

**Regarding "the last days," what good things does the Bible foretell?**

HAVE you watched the news on television and wondered, 'What is this world coming to?' Tragic things happen so suddenly and unexpectedly that no human can predict what tomorrow will bring. (James 4:14) However, Jehovah knows what the future holds. (Isaiah 46:10) Long ago his Word, the Bible, foretold not only the bad things happening in our day but also the wonderful things that will occur in the near future.

² Jesus Christ spoke about the Kingdom of God, which will bring an end to wickedness and make

1. Where can we learn about the future?
2, 3. What question did the disciples ask Jesus, and how did he reply?

the earth a paradise. (Luke 4:43) People wanted to know when the Kingdom would come. In fact, Jesus' disciples asked him: "What will be the sign of your presence and of the conclusion of the system of things?" (Matthew 24:3) In reply Jesus told them that only Jehovah God knew exactly when the end of this system of things would come. (Matthew 24:36) But Jesus did foretell things that would take place on earth just before the Kingdom would bring true peace and security to mankind. What he foretold is now taking place!

³ Before we examine the evidence that we are living in "the conclusion of the system of things," let us briefly consider a war that no human could possibly have observed. It took place in the invisible spirit realm, and its outcome affects us.

## A WAR IN HEAVEN

⁴ The preceding chapter in this book explained that Jesus Christ became King in heaven in the year 1914. (Daniel 7:13, 14) Soon after he received

**4, 5. (a) What took place in heaven soon after Jesus was enthroned as King? (b) According to Revelation 12:12, what was to be the result of the war in heaven?**

*What Does the Bible Really Teach?*

Kingdom power, Jesus took action. "War broke out in heaven," says the Bible. "Michael [another name for Jesus] and his angels battled with the dragon [Satan the Devil], and the dragon and its angels battled."* Satan and his wicked angels, the demons, lost that war and were cast out of heaven to the earth. God's faithful spirit sons rejoiced that Satan and his demons were gone. Humans, however, would experience no such joy. Instead, the Bible foretold: "Woe for the earth . . . because the Devil has come down to you, having great anger, knowing he has a short period of time."—Revelation 12:7, 9, 12.

5 Please notice what would result from the war in heaven. In his fury, Satan would bring woe, or trouble, upon those on earth. As you will see, we are now living in that time of woe. But it will be relatively brief—only "a short period of time." Even Satan realizes that. The Bible refers to this period as "the last days." (2 Timothy 3:1) How glad we can be that God will soon do away with the

---

* For information showing that Michael is another name for Jesus Christ, see the Appendix, pages 280-1.

Devil's influence over the earth! Let us consider some of the things foretold in the Bible that are happening right now. These prove that we are living in the last days and that God's Kingdom will soon bring everlasting blessings to those who love Jehovah. First, let us examine four features of the sign that Jesus said would mark the time in which we live.

## MAJOR DEVELOPMENTS OF THE LAST DAYS

Nars 1.

⁶ *"Nation will rise against nation and kingdom against kingdom."* (Matthew 24:7) Millions of people have been killed in wars during the past century. One British historian wrote: "The 20th century was the most murderous in recorded history. . . . It was a century of almost unbroken war, with few and brief periods without organised armed conflict somewhere." A report from the Worldwatch Institute states: "Three times as many people fell victim to war in [the 20th] century as in all the wars from the first century AD to 1899."

**6, 7. How are Jesus' words about wars and food shortages being fulfilled today?**

*What Does the Bible Really Teach?*

More than 100 million people have died as a result of wars since 1914. Even if we know the sorrow of losing *one* loved one in warfare, we can only imagine such misery and pain multiplied *millions* of times over.

2. [7] *"There will be food shortages."* (Matthew 24:7) Researchers say that food production has increased greatly during the past 30 years. Nevertheless, food shortages continue because many people do not have enough money to buy food or land on which to raise crops. In developing countries, well over a billion people have to live on an income of a dollar or less a day. The majority of these suffer from chronic hunger. The World Health Organization estimates that malnutrition plays a major role in the deaths of more than five million children each year.

3. [8] *"There will be great earthquakes."* (Luke 21:11) According to the U.S. Geological Survey, since 1990 alone an average of 17 earthquakes per

**8, 9. What shows that Jesus' prophecies about earthquakes and pestilences have come true?**

year have been powerful enough to damage buildings and crack the ground. And on an average, earthquakes strong enough to cause total destruction of buildings have occurred yearly. Another source states: "Earthquakes have claimed hundreds of thousands of lives in the last 100 years and improvements in technology have only slightly reduced the death toll."

*H.* ⁹ *"There will be . . . pestilences."* (Luke 21:11) Despite medical advances, old and new diseases plague mankind. One report says that 20 well-known diseases—including tuberculosis, malaria, and cholera—have become more common in recent decades, and some types of disease are increasingly difficult to cure by means of drugs. In fact, at least 30 new diseases have appeared. Some of them have no known cure and are fatal.

## PEOPLE OF THE LAST DAYS

¹⁰ Aside from identifying certain world developments, the Bible foretold that the last days would be marked by a change in human society. The

**10. What traits foretold at 2 Timothy 3:1-5 do you see in people today?**

*What Does the Bible Really Teach?*

apostle Paul described what people in general would be like. At 2 Timothy 3:1-5, we read: "In the last days critical times hard to deal with will be here." In part, Paul said that people would be

- *lovers of themselves*
- *lovers of money*
- *disobedient to parents*
- *disloyal*
- *having no natural affection*
- *without self-control*
- *fierce*
- *lovers of pleasures rather than lovers of God*
- *having a form of godly devotion but proving false to its power*

11 Have people become like that in your community? No doubt they have. There are people everywhere who have bad traits. This shows that God will soon act, for the Bible says: "When the wicked ones sprout as the vegetation and all the practicers of what is hurtful blossom forth, it is that they may be annihilated forever."—Psalm 92:7.

**11. How does Psalm 92:7 describe what will happen to the wicked ones?**

## POSITIVE DEVELOPMENTS!

**12** The last days are indeed filled with woe, just as the Bible foretold. In this troubled world, however, there are positive developments among the worshipers of Jehovah.

**13** *"The true knowledge will become abundant,"* the Bible book of Daniel foretold. When would that happen? During "the time of the end." (Daniel 12:4) Especially since 1914, Jehovah has helped those who truly desire to serve him to grow in understanding of the Bible. They have grown in appreciation of precious truths about God's name and purpose, the ransom sacrifice of Jesus Christ, the condition of the dead, and the resurrection. Moreover, worshipers of Jehovah have learned how to live their lives in a way that benefits them and brings praise to God. They have also gained a clearer understanding of the role of God's Kingdom and how it will set matters straight on the earth. What do they do with this

**12, 13. How has "true knowledge" become abundant in this "time of the end"?**

knowledge? That question brings us to yet another prophecy that is being fulfilled in these last days.

14 *"This good news of the kingdom will be preached in all the inhabited earth,"* said Jesus Christ in his prophecy about "the conclusion of the system of things." (Matthew 24:3, 14) Throughout the earth, the good news of the Kingdom—what the Kingdom is, what it will do, and how we can receive its blessings—is being preached in over 230 lands and in more than 400 languages. Millions of Jehovah's Witnesses zealously preach the Kingdom good news. They come from "all nations and tribes and peoples and tongues." (Revelation 7:9) The Witnesses conduct free home Bible studies with millions of people who want to know what the Bible really teaches. What an impressive fulfillment of prophecy, especially since Jesus foretold that true Christians would be "objects of hatred by all people"!—Luke 21:17.

**14. How widespread is the preaching of the Kingdom good news today, and who are preaching it?**

# WHAT WILL YOU DO? *tell us what to look for*

**15** Since so many Bible prophecies are being fulfilled today, do you not agree that we are living in the last days? After the good news is preached to Jehovah's satisfaction, "the end" is certain to come. (Matthew 24:14) "The end" means the time when God will get rid of wickedness on earth. To destroy all who willfully oppose Him, Jehovah will use Jesus and powerful angels. (2 Thessalonians 1: 6-9) Satan and his demons will no longer mislead the nations. After that, God's Kingdom will shower blessings upon all who submit to its righteous rulership.—Revelation 20:1-3; 21:3-5.

**16** Since the end of Satan's system is near, we need to ask ourselves, 'What should I be doing?' It is wise to continue to learn more about Jehovah and his requirements for us. (John 17:3) Be a serious student of the Bible. Make it your habit to associate regularly with others who seek to do Jehovah's will. (Hebrews 10:24, 25) Take in the

---

**15. (a)** Do you believe that we are living in the last days, and why? **(b)** What will "the end" mean for those who oppose Jehovah and for those who submit to the rulership of God's Kingdom?
**16.** What would it be wise for you to do?

*What Does the Bible Really Teach?*

abundant knowledge that Jehovah God has made available to people worldwide, and make necessary 3 changes in your life so that you may enjoy God's favor.—James 4:8.

17 Jesus foretold that most people would ignore the evidence that we are living in the last days. The destruction of the wicked will come suddenly and unexpectedly. Like a thief in the night, it will catch most people by surprise. (1 Thessalonians 5:2) Jesus warned: "As the days of Noah were, so the presence of the Son of man will be. For as they were in those days before the flood, eating and drinking, men marrying and women being given in marriage, until the day that Noah entered into the ark; and they took no note until the flood came and swept them all away, so the presence of the Son of man will be."—Matthew 24:37-39.

18 Hence, Jesus told his listeners: "Pay attention to yourselves that your hearts never become weighed down with overeating and heavy drinking and anxieties of life, and suddenly that day be

17. Why will the destruction of the wicked catch most people by surprise?
18. What warning by Jesus should we take to heart?

instantly upon you as a snare. For it will come in upon all those dwelling upon the face of all the earth. Keep awake, then, all the time making supplication that you may succeed in escaping all these things that are destined to occur, and in standing [with approval] before the Son of man." (Luke 21:34-36) It is wise to take Jesus' words to heart. Why? Because those having the approval of Jehovah God and "the Son of man," Jesus Christ, have the prospect of surviving the end of Satan's system of things and of living forever in the marvelous new world that is so close at hand!—John 3:16; 2 Peter 3:13.

---

### WHAT THE BIBLE TEACHES

- The last days are marked by wars, food shortages, earthquakes, and pestilences.—Matthew 24:7; Luke 21:11.

- In the last days, many love themselves, money, and pleasures but do not love God. —2 Timothy 3:1-5.

- During these last days, the good news of the Kingdom is being preached worldwide. —Matthew 24:14.

---

*What Does the Bible Really Teach?*

CHAPTER TEN

# Spirit Creatures—How They Affect Us

**Do angels help people?**

**How have wicked spirits influenced humans?**

**Do we need to fear wicked spirits?**

GETTING to know a person usually involves learning something about his family. Similarly, getting to know Jehovah God includes becoming better acquainted with his angelic family. The Bible calls the angels "sons of God." (Job 38:7) So, what is their place in God's purpose? Have they played a role in human history? Do angels affect your life? If so, how?

² The Bible refers to angels hundreds of times. Let us consider a few of these references to learn more about angels. Where did angels come from? Colossians 1:16 says: "By means of him [Jesus Christ] all other things were created in the heavens and upon the earth." Hence, all the spirit creatures called angels were individually created by Jehovah God

1. Why should we want to learn about angels?
2. Where did angels come from, and how many are there?

through his firstborn Son. How many angels are there? The Bible indicates that hundreds of millions of angels were created, and all of them are powerful. —Psalm 103:20.*

³ God's Word, the Bible, tells us that when the earth was founded, "all the sons of God began shouting in applause." (Job 38:4-7) Angels thus existed long before humans were created, even before the creation of the earth. This Bible passage also shows that angels have feelings, for it says that they *joyfully* cried out together." Note that *all* the sons of God" rejoiced *together.* At that time, all the angels were part of a united family serving Jehovah God.

## ANGELIC SUPPORT AND PROTECTION

⁴ Ever since they witnessed the creation of the first humans, faithful spirit creatures have shown keen interest in the growing human family and in the outworking of God's purpose. (Proverbs 8:30, 31; 1 Peter

---

* Regarding righteous angels, Revelation 5:11 says: "The number of them was myriads of myriads," or "ten thousand times tens of thousands." (Footnote) So the Bible does indicate that hundreds of millions of angels were created.

---

3. What does Job 38:4-7 tell us about angels?
4. How does the Bible show that faithful angels are interested in human activities?

*What Does the Bible Really Teach?*

1:11, 12) With the passing of time, however, the angels observed that most of the human family turned away from serving their loving Creator. No doubt this saddened the faithful angels. On the other hand, whenever even one human returns to Jehovah, "joy arises among the angels." (Luke 15:10) Since angels have such deep concern for the welfare of those who serve God, it is no wonder that Jehovah has repeatedly used angels to strengthen and protect his faithful servants on earth. (Hebrews 1:7, 14) Consider some examples.

5 Two angels helped the righteous man Lot and his daughters to survive the destruction of the wicked cities of Sodom and Gomorrah by leading them out of that area. (Genesis 19:15, 16) Centuries later, the prophet Daniel was thrown into a lions' pit, but he escaped harm and said: "My own God sent his angel and shut the mouth of the lions." (Daniel 6:22) In the first century C.E., an angel freed the apostle Peter from prison. (Acts 12:6-11) Moreover, angels supported Jesus at the start of his earthly ministry.

5. What examples of angelic support do we find in the Bible?

(Mark 1:13) And shortly before Jesus' death, an angel appeared to Jesus and "strengthened him." (Luke 22:43) What a comfort that must have been for Jesus at those very important times in his life!

6 Today, angels no longer appear visibly to God's people on earth. Although invisible to human eyes, God's powerful angels still protect his people, especially from anything spiritually harmful. The Bible says: "The angel of Jehovah is camping all around those fearing him, and he rescues them." (Psalm 34:7) Why should those words be of great comfort to us? Because there are dangerous wicked spirit creatures who want to destroy us! Who are they? Where do they come from? How are they trying to harm us? To find out, let us briefly consider something that happened at the start of human history.

## SPIRIT CREATURES WHO ARE OUR ENEMIES

7 As we learned in Chapter 3 of this book, one of the angels developed a desire to rule over others and thus turned against God. Later this angel became

6. (a) How do angels protect God's people today? (b) What questions will we now consider?
7. To what extent did Satan succeed in turning people away from God?

　　　　　　　*What Does the Bible Really Teach?*

known as Satan the Devil. (Revelation 12:9) During the 16 centuries after he deceived Eve, Satan succeeded in turning away from God nearly all humans except a few faithful ones, such as Abel, Enoch, and Noah.—Hebrews 11:4, 5, 7.

⁸ In Noah's day, other angels rebelled against Jehovah. They left their place in God's heavenly family, came down to the earth, and took on fleshly bodies. Why? We read at Genesis 6:2: "The sons of the true God began to notice the daughters of men, that they were good-looking; and they went taking wives for themselves, namely, all whom they chose." But Jehovah God did not allow the actions of these angels and the resulting corruption of mankind to go on. He brought upon the earth a global flood that swept away all wicked humans and preserved only his faithful servants. (Genesis 7:17, 23) Thus, the rebellious angels, or demons, were forced to abandon their fleshly bodies and return to heaven as spirit creatures. They put themselves on the side of the Devil, who became "the ruler of the demons."—Matthew 9:34.

**8. (a) How did some angels become demons? (b) To survive the Flood of Noah's day, what did the demons have to do?**

⁹ When the disobedient angels returned to heaven, they were treated as outcasts, like their ruler, Satan. (2 Peter 2:4) Although they are now unable to take on human bodies, they still exercise a very bad influence over humans. In fact, with the help of these demons, Satan "is misleading the entire inhabited earth." (Revelation 12:9; 1 John 5:19) How? Mainly, the demons use methods designed to mislead people. (2 Corinthians 2:11) Let us consider some of these methods.

## HOW DEMONS MISLEAD

¹⁰ To mislead people, the demons use spiritism. The practice of spiritism is involvement with the demons, both in a direct way and through a human medium. The Bible condemns spiritism and warns us to keep free from everything connected with it. (Galatians 5: 19-21) Spiritism does for the demons what bait does for fishermen. A fisherman uses a variety of baits to catch various kinds of fish. Similarly, wicked spirits use different forms of spiritism to bring all sorts of people under their influence.

9. (a) What happened to the demons when they returned to heaven? (b) We will consider what with regard to the demons?
10. What is spiritism?

*What Does the Bible Really Teach?*

**11** One type of bait used by the demons is divination. What is divination? It is an attempt to find out about the future or about something unknown. Some forms of divination are astrology, the use of tarot cards, crystal gazing, palmistry, and the search for mysterious omens, or signs, in dreams. Although many people think that practicing divination is harmless, the Bible shows that fortune-tellers and wicked spirits work together. For instance, Acts 16:16-18 mentions "a demon of divination" that enabled a girl to practice "the art of prediction." But she lost this ability when the demon was cast out of her.

**12** Another way that the demons mislead people is by encouraging them to inquire of the dead. People grieving over the death of a loved one are often deceived by wrong ideas about those who have died. A spirit medium may give special information or may speak in a voice that seems to be that of a dead person. As a result, many people become convinced that the dead are really alive and that contacting them will help the living to endure their grief. But any such

11. What is divination, and why should we avoid it?
12. Why is it dangerous to try to communicate with the dead?

## HOW TO RESIST WICKED SPIRITS

- Get rid of spiritistic items
- Study the Bible
- Pray to God

"comfort" is really false as well as dangerous. Why? Because the demons can imitate the voice of a dead person and give a spirit medium information about the one who died. (1 Samuel 28:3-19) Moreover, as we learned in Chapter 6, the dead have ceased to exist. (Psalm 115:17) So "anyone who inquires of the dead" has been misled by wicked spirits and is acting contrary to the will of God. (Deuteronomy 18:10, 11; Isaiah 8:19) Therefore, be careful to reject this dangerous bait used by the demons.

[13] Wicked spirits not only mislead people but also frighten them. Today, Satan and his demons know that they have only "a short period of time" left before they are put out of action, and they are now more vicious than ever. (Revelation 12:12, 17) Even so, thousands of people who once lived in daily dread of

13. What have many who once feared the demons been able to do?

*What Does the Bible Really Teach?*

such wicked spirits have been able to break free. How did they do this? What can a person do even if he is already involved in spiritism?

## HOW TO RESIST WICKED SPIRITS

14 The Bible tells us both how to resist wicked spirits and how to break free from them. Consider the example of the first-century Christians in the city of Ephesus. Some of them practiced spiritism before becoming Christians. When they decided to break free from spiritism, what did they do? The Bible says: "Quite a number of those who practiced magical arts brought their books together and burned them up before everybody." (Acts 19:19) By destroying their books on magic, those new Christians set an example for those who wish to resist wicked spirits today. People who want to serve Jehovah need to get rid of everything related to spiritism. That includes books, magazines, movies, posters, and music recordings that encourage the practice of spiritism and make it seem appealing and exciting. Included, too, are amulets or other items worn for protection against evil. —1 Corinthians 10:21.

14. Like the first-century Christians in Ephesus, how can we break free from wicked spirits?

**15** Some years after the Christians in Ephesus destroyed their books on magic, the apostle Paul wrote them: "We *have* a wrestling . . . against the wicked spirit forces." (Ephesians 6:12) The demons had not given up. They were still trying to gain an advantage. So, what else did those Christians need to do? "Above all things," said Paul, "take up the large shield of faith, with which you will be able to quench all the wicked one's [Satan's] burning missiles." (Ephesians 6:16) The stronger our shield of faith, the greater our resistance to wicked spirit forces will be.—Matthew 17:20.

**16** How, then, can we strengthen our faith? By studying the Bible. The firmness of a wall depends very much on the strength of its foundation. In the same way, the firmness of our faith depends greatly on the strength of its base, which is accurate knowledge of God's Word, the Bible. If we read and study the Bible daily, our faith will become strong. Like a strong wall, such faith will shield us from the influence of wicked spirits.—1 John 5:5.

---

15. To resist wicked spirit forces, what do we need to do?
16. How can we strengthen our faith?

*What Does the Bible Really Teach?*

**17** What other step did those Christians in Ephesus need to take? They needed further protection because they were living in a city filled with demonism. So Paul told them: "With every form of prayer and supplication . . . carry on prayer on every occasion in spirit." (Ephesians 6:18) Since we too live in a world full of demonism, earnestly praying to Jehovah for his protection is essential in resisting wicked spirits. Of course, we need to use Jehovah's name in our prayers. (Proverbs 18:10) Hence, we should keep on praying to God to "deliver us from the wicked one," Satan the Devil. (Matthew 6:13) Jehovah will answer such earnest prayers.—Psalm 145:19.

**18** Wicked spirits are dangerous, but we need not live in fear of them if we oppose the Devil and draw close to God by doing His will. (James 4:7, 8) The power of wicked spirits is limited. They were punished in Noah's day, and they face their final judgment in the future. (Jude 6) Remember, too, that we have the protection of Jehovah's powerful angels.

17. What step is necessary in order to resist wicked spirits?
18, 19. (a) Why can we be sure of victory in our fight against wicked spirit creatures? (b) What question will be answered in the next chapter?

(2 Kings 6:15-17) Those angels are deeply interested in seeing us succeed in resisting wicked spirits. The righteous angels are cheering us on, so to speak. Let us therefore stay close to Jehovah and his family of faithful spirit creatures. May we also avoid every kind of spiritism and always apply the counsel of God's Word. (1 Peter 5:6, 7; 2 Peter 2:9) Then we can be sure of victory in our fight against wicked spirit creatures.

[19] But why has God tolerated evil spirits and the wickedness that has caused people so much suffering? That question will be answered in the next chapter.

---

## WHAT THE BIBLE TEACHES

- Faithful angels come to the aid of those who serve Jehovah.—Hebrews 1:7, 14.

- Satan and his demons are misleading people and turning them away from God. —Revelation 12:9.

- If you do God's will and oppose the Devil, Satan will flee from you.—James 4:7, 8.

---

*What Does the Bible Really Teach?*

# CHAPTER ELEVEN

# Why Does God Allow Suffering?

**Has God caused the suffering in the world?**

**What issue was raised in the garden of Eden?**

**How will God undo the effects of human suffering?**

AFTER a terrible battle in one war-torn land, the thousands of civilian women and children who had been killed were buried in a mass grave surrounded by markers. Each marker bore this inscription: "Why?" Sometimes that is the most painful question of all. People ask it sadly when war, disaster, disease, or crime takes their innocent loved ones, destroys their home, or brings them untold suffering in other ways. They want to know why such tragedies befall them.

² Why does God allow suffering? If Jehovah God is all-powerful, loving, wise, and just, why is the world

---

**1, 2. What kind of suffering do people face today, leading many to ask what questions?**

so full of hatred and injustice? Have you ever wondered about these things yourself?

3 Is it wrong to ask why God allows suffering? Some worry that asking such a question means that they do not have enough faith or that they are showing disrespect for God. When reading the Bible, however, you will find that faithful, God-fearing people had similar questions. For example, the prophet Habakkuk asked Jehovah: "Why is it that you make me see what is hurtful, and you keep looking upon mere trouble? And why are despoiling and violence in front of me, and why does quarreling occur, and why is strife carried?"—Habakkuk 1:3.

4 Did Jehovah scold the faithful prophet Habakkuk for asking such questions? No. Instead, God included Habakkuk's sincere words in the inspired Bible record. God also helped him to get a clearer understanding of matters and to gain greater faith. Jehovah wants to do the same for you. Remember, the Bible teaches that "he cares for you." (1 Peter 5:7) God hates wickedness and the suffering it causes far more

3, 4. (a) What shows that it is not wrong to ask why God allows suffering? (b) How does Jehovah feel about wickedness and suffering?

*What Does the Bible Really Teach?*

than any human does. (Isaiah 55:8, 9) Why, then, is there so much suffering in the world?

## WHY SO MUCH SUFFERING?

5 People of various religions have gone to their religious leaders and teachers to ask why there is so much suffering. Often, the response is that suffering is God's will and that he long ago determined everything that would ever happen, including tragic events. Many are told that God's ways are mysterious or that he brings death upon people—even children—so that he can have them in heaven with him. As you have learned, though, Jehovah God never causes what is bad. The Bible says: "Far be it from the true God to act wickedly, and the Almighty to act unjustly!"—Job 34:10.

6 Do you know why people make the mistake of blaming God for all the suffering in the world? In many cases, they blame Almighty God because they think that he is the real ruler of this world. They do

5. What reasons are sometimes offered to explain human suffering, but what does the Bible teach?
6. Why do many people make the mistake of blaming God for the suffering in the world?

not know a simple but important truth that the Bible teaches. You learned that truth in Chapter 3 of this book. The real ruler of this world is Satan the Devil.

7 The Bible clearly states: "The whole world is lying in the power of the wicked one." (1 John 5:19) When you think about it, does that not make sense? This world reflects the personality of the invisible spirit creature who is "misleading the entire inhabited earth." (Revelation 12:9) Satan is hateful, deceptive, and cruel. So the world, under his influence, is full of hatred, deceit, and cruelty. That is one reason why there is so much suffering.

8 A second reason why there is so much suffering is that, as discussed in Chapter 3, mankind has been imperfect and sinful ever since the rebellion in the garden of Eden. Sinful humans tend to struggle for dominance, and this results in wars, oppression, and suffering. (Ecclesiastes 4:1; 8:9) A third reason for suffering is "time and unforeseen occurrence." (Ecclesiastes 9:11) In a world without Jehovah as a protec-

7, 8. (a) How does the world reflect the personality of its ruler? (b) How have human imperfection and "time and unforeseen occurrence" contributed to suffering?

tive Ruler, people may suffer because they happen to be in the wrong place at the wrong time.

⁹ It is comforting for us to know that God does not cause suffering. He is not responsible for the wars, the crimes, the oppression, or even the natural disasters that cause people to suffer. Still, we need to know, Why does Jehovah allow all this suffering? If he is the Almighty, he has the power to stop it. Why, then, does he hold back? The loving God that we have come to know must have a good reason.—1 John 4:8.

## A VITAL ISSUE IS RAISED  *11-14-10*

¹⁰ To find out why God allows suffering, we need to think back to the time when suffering began. When Satan led Adam and Eve into disobeying Jehovah, an important question was raised. Satan did not call into question Jehovah's *power*. Even Satan knows that there is no limit to Jehovah's power. Rather, Satan questioned Jehovah's *right to rule*. By calling God a liar who withholds good from his subjects, Satan charged that Jehovah is a bad ruler. (Genesis 3:

**9.** Why can we be sure that Jehovah has a good reason for allowing suffering to continue?
**10.** What did Satan call into question, and how?

2-5) Satan implied that mankind would be better off without God's rulership. This was an attack on Jehovah's *sovereignty,* his right to rule.

[11] Adam and Eve rebelled against Jehovah. In effect, they said: "We do not need Jehovah as our Ruler. We can decide for ourselves what is right and what is wrong." How could Jehovah settle that issue? How could he teach all intelligent creatures that the rebels were wrong and that his way truly is best? Someone might say that God should simply have destroyed the rebels and made a fresh start. But Jehovah had stated his purpose to fill the earth with the offspring of Adam and Eve, and he wanted them to live in an earthly paradise. (Genesis 1:28) Jehovah *always* fulfills his purposes. (Isaiah 55:10, 11) Besides that, getting rid of the rebels in Eden would not have answered the question that had been raised regarding Jehovah's right to rule.

[12] Let us consider an illustration. Imagine that a teacher is telling his students how to solve a difficult

11. Why did Jehovah not just destroy the rebels in Eden?
12, 13. Illustrate why Jehovah has allowed Satan to become the ruler of this world and why God has permitted humans to govern themselves.

*What Does the Bible Really Teach?*

problem. A clever but rebellious student claims that the teacher's way of solving the problem is wrong. Implying that the teacher is not capable, this rebel insists that he knows a much better way to solve the problem. Some students think that he is right, and they also become rebellious. What should the teacher do? If he throws the rebels out of the class, what will be the effect on the other students? Will they not believe that their fellow student and those who joined him are right? All the other students in the class might lose respect for the teacher, thinking that he is afraid of being proved wrong. But suppose that the teacher allows the rebel to show the class how *he* would solve the problem.

¹³ Jehovah has done something similar to what the teacher does. Remember that the rebels in Eden were not the only ones involved. Millions of angels were watching. (Job 38:7; Daniel 7:10) How Jehovah handled the rebellion would greatly affect all those angels and eventually all intelligent creation. So, what has Jehovah done? He has allowed Satan to show how he would rule mankind. God has also allowed humans to govern themselves under Satan's guidance.

**14** The teacher in our illustration knows that the rebel and the students on his side are wrong. But he also knows that allowing them the opportunity to try to prove their point will benefit the whole class. When the rebels fail, all honest students will see that the teacher is the only one qualified to lead the class. They will understand why the teacher thereafter removes any rebels from the class. Similarly, Jehovah knows that all honesthearted humans and angels will benefit from seeing that Satan and his fellow rebels have failed and that humans cannot govern themselves. Like Jeremiah of old, they will learn this vital truth: "I well know, O Jehovah, that to earthling man his way does not belong. It does not belong to man who is walking even to direct his step."—Jeremiah 10:23.

*Daniel 7:10*

*1-5-11*

## WHY SO LONG?

**15** Why, though, has Jehovah allowed suffering to go on for so long? And why does he not prevent bad

**14. What benefit will come from Jehovah's decision to allow humans to govern themselves?**
**15, 16. (a) Why has Jehovah allowed suffering to continue for so long? (b) Why has Jehovah not prevented such things as horrible crimes?**

things from happening? Well, consider two things that the teacher in our illustration would *not* do. First, he would not stop the rebel student from presenting his case. Second, the teacher would not help the rebel to make his case. Similarly, consider two things that Jehovah has determined *not* to do. First, he has not stopped Satan and those who side with him from trying to prove that they are right. Allowing time to pass has thus been necessary. In the thousands of years of human history, mankind has been able to try every form of self-rule, or human government. Mankind has made some advances in science and other fields, but injustice, poverty, crime, and war have grown ever worse. Human rule has now been *shown* to be a failure.

¹⁶ Second, Jehovah has not helped Satan to rule this world. If God were to prevent horrible crimes, for instance, would he not, in effect, be supporting the case of the rebels? Would God not be making people think that perhaps humans *can* govern themselves without disastrous results? If Jehovah were to act in that way, he would become party to a lie. However, "it is impossible for God to lie."—Hebrews 6:18.

**17** What, though, about all the harm that has been done during the long rebellion against God? We do well to remember that Jehovah is almighty. Therefore, he can and will undo the effects of mankind's suffering. As we have already learned, the ruining of our planet will be undone by the turning of the earth into Paradise. The effects of sin will be removed through faith in Jesus' ransom sacrifice, and the effects of death will be reversed by means of the resurrection. God will thus use Jesus "to break up the works of the Devil." (1 John 3:8) Jehovah will bring all of this about at just the right time. We can be glad that he has not acted sooner, for his patience has given us the opportunity to learn the truth and to serve him. (2 Peter 3:9, 10) Meanwhile, God has been actively seeking sincere worshipers and helping them to endure any suffering that may come upon them in this troubled world.—John 4:23; 1 Corinthians 10:13.

**18** Some might wonder, Could all this suffering have been prevented if God had created Adam and Eve in such a way that they *could not* rebel? To answer that

**17, 18. What will Jehovah do about all the harm that has resulted from the rule of humans and the influence of Satan?**

*What Does the Bible Really Teach?*

question, you need to remember a precious gift that Jehovah has given you.

## HOW WILL YOU USE THE GIFT FROM GOD?

19 As was noted in Chapter 5, humans were created with free will. Do you realize what a precious gift that is? God has made countless animals, and these are driven largely by instinct. (Proverbs 30:24) Man has made some robots that can be programmed to follow every command. Would we be happy if God had made us like that? No, we are glad to have the freedom to make choices about what kind of person to become, what course of life to pursue, what friendships to form, and so on. We love to have a measure of freedom, and that is what God wants us to enjoy.

20 Jehovah is not interested in service performed under compulsion. (2 Corinthians 9:7) To illustrate: What would please a parent more—a child's saying "I love you" because he is told to say it or his saying it freely from the heart? So the question is, How will

19. What precious gift has Jehovah given us, and why should we value it?

20, 21. How may we use the gift of free will in the best possible way, and why should we want to do so?

*you* use the free will that Jehovah has given you? Satan, Adam, and Eve made the worst possible use of free will. They rejected Jehovah God. What will you do?

**21** You have the opportunity to put the marvelous gift of free will to the best possible use. You can join the millions who have taken a stand on Jehovah's side. They make God rejoice because they take an active part in proving Satan a liar and a miserable failure as a ruler. (Proverbs 27:11) You too can do that by choosing the right course of life. This will be explained in the next chapter.

---

### WHAT THE BIBLE TEACHES

- God does not cause the bad conditions in the world.—Job 34:10.

- By calling God a liar and saying that He withholds good from His subjects, Satan questioned Jehovah's right to rule. —Genesis 3:2-5.

- Jehovah will use his Son, the Ruler of the Messianic Kingdom, to end all human suffering and to undo its effects.—1 John 3:8.

---

*What Does the Bible Really Teach?*

# CHAPTER TWELVE

# Living in a Way That Pleases God

**How can you become God's friend?**

**In what way does Satan's challenge involve you?**

**What conduct displeases Jehovah?**

**How can you live in a way that pleases God?**

WHAT kind of person would you choose as a friend? Very likely you would want the company of someone who shares your views, interests, and values. And you would be drawn to one who has fine qualities, such as honesty and kindness.

² Throughout history, God has chosen certain humans to be his close friends. For example, Jehovah called Abraham his friend. (Isaiah 41:8; James 2:23) God referred to David as "a man agreeable to my heart" because he was the kind of person Jehovah loves. (Acts 13:22) And Jehovah viewed the prophet Daniel as "someone very desirable."—Daniel 9:23.

**1, 2. Give some examples of humans whom Jehovah viewed as his close friends.**

³ Why did Jehovah consider Abraham, David, and Daniel to be his friends? Well, he told Abraham: "You have listened to my voice." (Genesis 22:18) So Jehovah draws close to those who humbly do what he asks of them. "Obey my voice," he told the Israelites, "and I will become your God, and you yourselves will become my people." (Jeremiah 7:23) If you obey Jehovah, you too can become his friend!

## JEHOVAH STRENGTHENS HIS FRIENDS

⁴ Think about what friendship with God means. The Bible says that Jehovah is looking for opportunities "to show his strength in behalf of those whose heart is complete toward him." (2 Chronicles 16:9) How can Jehovah show his strength in your behalf? One way is brought out at Psalm 32:8, where we read: "I [Jehovah] shall make you have insight and instruct you in the way you should go. I will give advice with my eye upon you."

⁵ What a touching expression of Jehovah's care! He will give you needed direction and watch over you as you apply it. God *wants* to help you get through

3. Why does Jehovah choose certain humans to be his friends?
4, 5. How does Jehovah show his strength in behalf of his people?

your trials and tests. (Psalm 55:22) So if you serve Jehovah with a complete heart, you can be as confident as the psalmist who said: "I have placed Jehovah in front of me constantly. Because he is at my right hand, I shall not be made to totter." (Psalm 16:8; 63:8) Yes, Jehovah can help you to live in a way that pleases him. But, as you know, there is an enemy of God who would like to keep you from doing this.

## SATAN'S CHALLENGE

⁶ Chapter 11 of this book explained how Satan the Devil challenged God's sovereignty. Satan charged God with lying and implied that Jehovah was unfair in not letting Adam and Eve decide for themselves what was right and what was wrong. After Adam and Eve sinned and as the earth began to be filled with their offspring, Satan questioned the motive of all humans. "People do not serve God because they love him," Satan charged. "Give me a chance, and I can turn *anyone* against God." The account of the man named Job shows that this is what Satan

**6. What was Satan's charge regarding humans?**

believed. Who was Job, and how was he involved with Satan's challenge?

7 Job lived about 3,600 years ago. He was a good man, for Jehovah said: "There is no one like him in the earth, a man blameless and upright, fearing God and turning aside from bad." (Job 1:8) Job was pleasing to God.

8 Satan questioned Job's motive for serving God. The Devil said to Jehovah: "Have not you yourself put up a hedge about [Job] and about his house and about everything that he has all around? The work of his hands you have blessed, and his livestock itself has spread abroad in the earth. But, for a change, thrust out your hand, please, and touch everything he has and see whether he will not curse you to your very face."—Job 1:10, 11.

9 Satan thus argued that Job served God just for what he got in return. The Devil also charged that if Job was tested, he would turn against God. How

7, 8. (a) What made Job outstanding among humans of that time? (b) How did Satan call Job's motive into question?
9. How did Jehovah respond to Satan's challenge, and why?

*What Does the Bible Really Teach?*

did Jehovah respond to Satan's challenge? Since the issue involved Job's motive, Jehovah allowed Satan to test Job. In this way, Job's love for God—or lack of it—would be clearly shown.

## JOB IS TESTED

10 Satan soon tested Job in a number of ways. Some of Job's animals were stolen, and others were killed. Most of his servants were slaughtered. This brought economic hardship. Further tragedy struck when Job's ten children died in a storm. Despite these terrible events, however, "Job did not sin or ascribe anything improper to God."—Job 1:22.

11 Satan did not give up. He must have thought that although Job could endure the loss of his possessions, servants, and children, he would turn against God if he became sick. Jehovah let Satan strike Job with a disgusting, painful disease. But even this did not cause Job to lose faith in God. Rather, he firmly said: "Until I expire I shall not take away my integrity!"—Job 27:5.

10. What trials befell Job, and how did he react?
11. (a) What second accusation did Satan make concerning Job, and how did Jehovah respond? (b) How did Job react to his painful disease?

¹² Job was not aware that Satan was the cause of his troubles. Not knowing the details about the Devil's challenge of Jehovah's sovereignty, Job feared that God was the source of his problems. (Job 6:4; 16:11-14) Still, he kept his integrity to Jehovah. And Satan's claim that Job served God for selfish reasons was proved false by Job's faithful course!

¹³ Job's faithfulness provided Jehovah with a forceful reply to Satan's insulting challenge. Job truly was Jehovah's friend, and God rewarded him for his faithful course.—Job 42:12-17.

## HOW YOU ARE INVOLVED

¹⁴ The issue of integrity to God that was raised by Satan was not directed against Job alone. You too are involved. This is clearly shown at Proverbs 27: 11, where Jehovah's Word says: "Be wise, my son, and make my heart rejoice, that I may make a reply to him that is taunting me." These words, written hundreds of years after Job's death, show that

12. How did Job answer the Devil's challenge?
13. What happened because Job was faithful to God?
14, 15. Why can we say that Satan's challenge involving Job applies to *all* humans?

*What Does the Bible Really Teach?*

Satan was still taunting God and accusing His servants. When we live in a way that pleases Jehovah, we actually help to give an answer to Satan's false charges, and in that way we make God's heart rejoice. How do you feel about that? Would it not be wonderful to have a part in answering the Devil's lying claims, even if it means making certain changes in your life?

15 Notice that Satan said: "Everything that *a man* has he will give in behalf of his soul." (Job 2:4) By saying "a man," Satan made it clear that his charge applied not just to Job but to *all* humans. That is a very important point. Satan has called into question *your* integrity to God. The Devil would like to see you disobey God and abandon a righteous course when difficulties arise. How might Satan try to accomplish this?

16 As discussed in Chapter 10, Satan uses various methods to try to turn people away from God. On the one hand, he attacks "like a roaring lion, seeking to devour someone." (1 Peter 5:8) Thus Satan's

16. (a) By what methods does Satan try to turn people away from God? (b) How might the Devil use these methods against you?

influence may be seen when friends, relatives, or others oppose your efforts to study the Bible and apply what you learn.* (John 15:19, 20) On the other hand, Satan "keeps transforming himself into an angel of light." (2 Corinthians 11:14) The Devil can use subtle means to mislead you and lure you away from a godly way of life. He can also use discouragement, perhaps causing you to feel that you are not good enough to please God. (Proverbs 24:10) Whether Satan is acting like "a roaring lion" or posing as "an angel of light," his challenge remains-the same: He says that when you are faced with trials or temptations, you will stop serving God. How can you answer his challenge and prove your integrity to God, as Job did?

## OBEYING JEHOVAH'S COMMANDMENTS

<sup>17</sup> You can answer Satan's challenge by living in a way that pleases God. What does this involve? The

* This does not mean that those who oppose you are personally controlled by Satan. But Satan is the god of this system of things, and the whole world is in his power. (2 Corinthians 4:4; 1 John 5: 19) So we can expect that living a godly life will be an unpopular course, and some will oppose you.

**17. What is the main reason to obey Jehovah's commandments?**

*What Does the Bible Really Teach?*

Bible answers: "You must love Jehovah your God with all your heart and all your soul and all your vital force." (Deuteronomy 6:5) As your love for God grows, you will be filled with a desire to do what he requires of you. "This is what the love of God means," wrote the apostle John, "that we observe his commandments." If you love Jehovah with your whole heart, you will find that "his commandments are not burdensome."—1 John 5:3.

18 What are Jehovah's commandments? Some of them involve conduct that we must avoid. For example, note the box on page 155, entitled "Shun What Jehovah Hates." There you will find listed conduct that the Bible clearly condemns. At first glance, some practices that are listed might not seem so bad. But after meditating on the cited scriptures, you will likely see the wisdom of Jehovah's laws. Making changes in your conduct may be the greatest challenge you have ever faced. Yet, living in a way that pleases God brings great satisfaction and happiness.

18, 19. (a) What are some of Jehovah's commandments? (See box on page 155.) (b) How do we know that God is not asking too much of us?

(Isaiah 48:17, 18) And it is something that is within your reach. How do we know that?

[19] Jehovah never asks more of us than we can do. (Deuteronomy 30:11-14) He knows our potential and our limitations better than we do. (Psalm 103:14) Moreover, Jehovah can give us the strength to obey him. The apostle Paul wrote: "God is faithful, and he will not let you be tempted beyond what you can bear, but along with the temptation he will also make the way out in order for you to be able to endure it." (1 Corinthians 10:13) To help you endure, Jehovah can even supply you with "power beyond what is normal." (2 Corinthians 4:7) After enduring many trials, Paul could say: "For all things I have the strength by virtue of him who imparts power to me."—Philippians 4:13.

## DEVELOPING GODLY QUALITIES

[20] Of course, more is involved in pleasing Jehovah than avoiding things that he hates. You also need to love what he loves. (Romans 12:9) Do you not feel drawn to those who share your views, interests,

20. What godly qualities should you develop, and why are these important?

*What Does the Bible Really Teach?*

# SHUN WHAT JEHOVAH HATES

*(handwritten: 12)*

**Manslaughter.**—Exodus 20:13; 21:22, 23. *(handwritten: Not Kill)*

**Sexual immorality.**—Leviticus 20:10, 13, 15, 16; *(handwritten: No adultery)*
Romans 1:24, 26, 27, 32; 1 Corinthians 6:9, 10.

**Spiritism.**—Deuteronomy 18:9-13; *(handwritten: No other Gods)*
1 Corinthians 10:21, 22; Galatians 5:20, 21.

**Idolatry.**—1 Corinthians 10:14. *(handwritten: No False idols)*

**Drunkenness.**—1 Corinthians 5:11.

**Stealing.**—Leviticus 6:2, 4; Ephesians 4:28. *(handwritten: No coveting)*

**Lying.**—Proverbs 6:16, 19; Colossians 3:9;
Revelation 22:15. *(handwritten: Not bear false witness)*

**Greed.**—1 Corinthians 5:11.

**Violence.**—Psalm 11:5; Proverbs 22:24, 25; *(handwritten: Peace)*
Malachi 2:16; Galatians 5:20.

**Improper speech.**—Leviticus 19:16; *(handwritten: No Holy on speech)*
Ephesians 5:4; Colossians 3:8.

**Misuse of blood.**
—Genesis 9:4; Acts 15:20, 28, 29.

**Refusal to provide for one's family.**
—1 Timothy 5:8.

**Participation in wars or political controversies** *(handwritten: Peace)*
**of this world.**—Isaiah 2:4; John 6:15; 17:16.

**Use of tobacco or so-called recreational drugs.**
—Mark 15:23; 2 Corinthians 7:1.

---

and values? Jehovah does too. So learn to love the things that Jehovah holds dear. Some of these are described at Psalm 15:1-5, where we read about those whom God considers his friends. Jehovah's friends display what the Bible calls "the fruitage of the spirit." It includes such qualities as "love, joy, peace, long-suffering, kindness, goodness, faith, mildness, self-control."—Galatians 5:22, 23.

21 Reading and studying the Bible regularly will help you to develop godly qualities. And learning what God requires will help you to harmonize your thoughts with God's thinking. (Isaiah 30:20, 21) The more you strengthen your love for Jehovah, the greater will be your desire to live in a way that pleases God.

22 Effort is required to live in a way that pleases Jehovah. The Bible likens changing your life to stripping off your old personality and clothing yourself with a new one. (Colossians 3:9, 10) But regarding Jehovah's commandments, the psalmist wrote: "In

**21. What will help you to develop godly qualities?**
**22. What will you accomplish if you live in a way that pleases God?**

*What Does the Bible Really Teach?*

the keeping of them there is a large reward." (Psalm 19:11) You too will find that living in a way that pleases God is richly rewarding. By so doing, you will give an answer to Satan's challenge and make Jehovah's heart rejoice!

---

### WHAT THE BIBLE TEACHES

- You can become God's friend by obeying him. —James 2:23.

- Satan has challenged the integrity of all humans.—Job 1:8, 10, 11; 2:4; Proverbs 27:11.

- We must shun practices that displease God.—1 Corinthians 6:9, 10.

- We can please Jehovah by hating what he hates and loving what he loves.—Romans 12:9.

---

# CHAPTER THIRTEEN

# A Godly View of Life

## How does God view life?

## How does God view abortion?

## How do we show respect for life?

"JEHOVAH is in truth God," said the prophet Jeremiah. "He is the living God." (Jeremiah 10:10) Furthermore, Jehovah God is the Creator of all living things. Heavenly creatures said to him: "You created all things, and because of your will they existed and were created." (Revelation 4:11) In a song of praise to God, King David said: "With you is the source of life." (Psalm 36:9) Life, then, is a gift from God.

² Jehovah also sustains our lives. (Acts 17:28) He provides the food we eat, the water we drink, the air we breathe, and the land we live on. (Acts 14:15-17) Jehovah has done this in a way that makes life

**1. Who created all living things?**
**2. What does God do to sustain our lives?**

enjoyable. But to enjoy life to the full, we need to learn God's laws and obey them.—Isaiah 48:17, 18.

## SHOWING RESPECT FOR LIFE

3 God wants us to have respect for life—both our own and that of others. Back in the days of Adam and Eve, for example, their son Cain became very angry with his younger brother Abel. Jehovah warned Cain that his anger could lead him to serious sin. Cain ignored that warning. He 'assaulted Abel his brother and killed him.' (Genesis 4:3-8) Jehovah punished Cain for murdering his brother. —Genesis 4:9-11.

4 Thousands of years later, Jehovah gave the people of Israel laws to help them to serve him acceptably. Because these laws were given through the prophet Moses, they are sometimes called the Mosaic Law. Part of the Mosaic Law said: "You must not murder." (Deuteronomy 5:17) This showed the Israelites that God values human life and that people must value the lives of others.

3. How did God view the murder of Abel?
4. In the Mosaic Law, how did God stress the proper view of life?

## WE SHOW RESPECT FOR LIFE

- by not taking the life of an unborn child
- by giving up unclean habits
- by rooting out of our heart any hatred for our fellowman

⁵ What about the life of an unborn child? Well, according to the Mosaic Law, causing the death of a baby in its mother's womb was wrong. Yes, even such a life is precious to Jehovah. (Exodus 21: 22, 23; Psalm 127:3) This means that abortion is wrong.

⁶ Having respect for life includes having the right view of fellow humans. The Bible says: "Everyone who hates his brother is a manslayer, and you know that no manslayer has everlasting life remaining in him." (1 John 3:15) If we want everlasting life, we need to root out of our heart any hatred for our fellowman, because hatred is the root cause

5. How should we view abortion?
6. Why should we not hate our fellowman?

*What Does the Bible Really Teach?*

of most violence. (1 John 3:11, 12) It is vital that we learn to love one another.

7 What about showing respect for our own life? People normally do not want to die, but some risk death for the sake of pleasure. For example, many use tobacco, chew betel nut, or take drugs for recreational purposes. Such substances harm the body and often kill the users. A person who makes it a practice to use these substances does not view life as sacred. These practices are unclean in God's eyes. (Romans 6:19; 12:1; 2 Corinthians 7:1) To serve God acceptably, we have to give up such practices. Although doing so might be very hard, Jehovah can give us the needed help. And he appreciates the effort we make to treat our life as a precious gift from him.

8 If we have respect for life, we will keep in mind the need to be safety conscious. We will not be careless and will not take risks just for pleasure or excitement. We will avoid reckless driving and violent or dangerous sports. (Psalm 11:5) God's law

7. What are some practices that show a disrespect for life?
8. Why should we keep in mind the need to be safety conscious?

for ancient Israel stated: "In case you build a new house [with a flat roof], you must also make a parapet [or, low wall] for your roof, that you may not place bloodguilt upon your house because someone falling might fall from it." (Deuteronomy 22:8) In harmony with the principle set out in that law, keep such things as stairs in good condition in your home so that someone does not trip, fall, and get badly hurt. If you own a car, make sure that it is safe to drive. Do not let either your home or your car be a danger to you or to others.

⁹ What about the life of an animal? That too is sacred to the Creator. God permits the killing of animals to obtain food and clothing or to protect people from danger. (Genesis 3:21; 9:3; Exodus 21:28) However, being cruel to animals or killing them just for sport is wrong and shows utter disregard for the sacredness of life.—Proverbs 12:10.

## SHOWING RESPECT FOR BLOOD
¹⁰ After Cain killed his brother Abel, Jehovah told Cain: "Your brother's blood is crying out to

**9.** If we have respect for life, how will we treat animals?
**10.** How has God shown that there is a link between life and blood?

*What Does the Bible Really Teach?*

me from the ground." (Genesis 4:10) When God spoke of Abel's blood, he was speaking of Abel's life. Cain had taken Abel's life, and now Cain would have to be punished. It was as if Abel's blood, or life, were crying out to Jehovah for justice. The connection between life and blood was again shown after the Flood of Noah's day. Before the Flood, humans ate only fruits, vegetables, grains, and nuts. After the Flood, Jehovah told Noah and his sons: "Every moving animal that is alive may serve as food for you. As in the case of green vegetation, I do give it all to you." However, God set this restriction: "Only flesh with its soul [or, life]—its blood—you must not eat." (Genesis 1: 29; 9:3, 4) Clearly, Jehovah links very closely the life and the blood of a creature.

¹¹ We show respect for blood by not eating it. In the Law that Jehovah gave the Israelites, he commanded: "As for any man . . . who in hunting catches a wild beast or a fowl that may be eaten, he must in that case pour its blood out and cover

11. **What use of blood has God forbidden since the days of Noah?**

it with dust. . . . I said to the sons of Israel: 'You must not eat the blood of any sort of flesh.'" (Leviticus 17:13, 14) God's command not to eat animal blood, first given to Noah some 800 years earlier, was still in force. Jehovah's view was clear: His servants could eat animal meat but not the blood. They were to pour the blood on the ground—in effect, returning the creature's life to God.

¹² A similar command rests upon Christians. The apostles and other men taking the lead among Jesus' followers in the first century met together to decide what commands had to be obeyed by all in the Christian congregation. They came to this conclusion: "The holy spirit and we ourselves have favored adding no further burden to you, except these necessary things, to keep abstaining from things sacrificed to idols and from blood and from things strangled [leaving the blood in the meat] and from fornication." (Acts 15:28, 29; 21:25) So we must 'keep abstaining from blood.' In God's eyes,

**12. What command regarding blood was given by holy spirit in the first century and still applies today?**

*What Does the Bible Really Teach?*

our doing that is as important as our avoiding idolatry and sexual immorality.

¹³ Does the command to abstain from blood include blood transfusions? Yes. To illustrate: Suppose a doctor were to tell you to abstain from alcoholic beverages. Would that simply mean that you should not drink alcohol but that you could have it injected into your veins? Of course not! Likewise, abstaining from blood means not taking it into our bodies at all. So the command to abstain from blood means that we would not allow anyone to transfuse blood into our veins.

¹⁴ What if a Christian is badly injured or is in need of major surgery? Suppose doctors say that he must have a blood transfusion or he will die. Of course, the Christian would not want to die. In an effort to preserve God's precious gift of life, he would accept other kinds of treatment that do not involve the misuse of blood. Hence, he would

13. Illustrate why the command to abstain from blood includes blood transfusions.
14, 15. If doctors say that a Christian must have a blood transfusion, how would he react, and why?

seek such medical attention if that is available and would accept a variety of alternatives to blood.

15 Would a Christian break God's law just to stay alive a little longer in this system of things? Jesus said: "Whoever wants to save his soul [or, life] will lose it; but whoever loses his soul for my sake will find it." (Matthew 16:25) We do not want to die. But if we tried to save our present life by breaking God's law, we would be in danger of losing everlasting life. We are wise, then, to put our trust in the rightness of God's law, with full confidence that if we die from any cause, our Life-Giver will remember us in the resurrection and restore to us the precious gift of life.—John 5:28, 29; Hebrews 11:6.

16 Today, faithful servants of God firmly resolve to follow his direction regarding blood. They will not eat it in any form. Nor will they accept blood for medical reasons.* They are sure that the Cre-

_____

* For information on alternatives to blood transfusion, see pages 13-17 of the brochure *How Can Blood Save Your Life?* published by Jehovah's Witnesses.

_____

**16. What do God's servants firmly resolve regarding blood?**

*What Does the Bible Really Teach?*

ator of blood knows what is best for them. Do you believe that he does?

## THE ONLY PROPER USE OF BLOOD

17 The Mosaic Law emphasized the one proper use of blood. Regarding the worship required of the ancient Israelites, Jehovah commanded: "The soul [or, life] of the flesh is in the blood, and I myself have put it upon the altar for you to make atonement for your souls, because it is the blood that makes atonement." (Leviticus 17:11) When the Israelites sinned, they could obtain forgiveness by offering an animal and having some of its blood put on the altar at the tabernacle or later at God's temple. The only proper use of blood was in such sacrifices.

18 True Christians are not under the Mosaic Law and therefore do not offer animal sacrifices and put the blood of animals on an altar. (Hebrews 10:1) However, the use of blood on the altar in the

17. In ancient Israel, what was the one use of blood that was acceptable to Jehovah God?
18. What benefits and blessings can we gain from the shedding of Jesus' blood?

days of ancient Israel pointed forward to the precious sacrifice of God's Son, Jesus Christ. As we learned in Chapter 5 of this book, Jesus gave his human life for us by letting his blood be shed as a sacrifice. Then he ascended to heaven and once for all time offered the value of his shed blood to God. (Hebrews 9:11, 12) That laid the basis for the forgiveness of our sins and opened the way for us to gain everlasting life. (Matthew 20:28; John 3:16) How extremely important that use of blood has proved to be! (1 Peter 1:18, 19) Only by means of faith in the merit of Jesus' shed blood can we gain salvation.

¹⁹ We can be so grateful to Jehovah God for the loving provision of life! And should that not motivate us to tell others about the opportunity to gain everlasting life on the basis of faith in Jesus' sacrifice? Godly concern for the lives of fellow humans will move us to do this with eagerness and zeal. (Ezekiel 3:17-21) If we diligently fulfill this responsibility, we will be able to say, as did the apostle

**19. What must we do in order to be "clean from the blood of all men"?**

*What Does the Bible Really Teach?*

Paul: "I am clean from the blood of all men, for I have not held back from telling you all the counsel of God." (Acts 20:26, 27) Telling people about God and his purposes is a fine way to show that we have the highest regard for life and blood.

---

## WHAT THE BIBLE TEACHES

- Life is a gift from God.—Psalm 36:9; Revelation 4:11.

- Abortion is wrong, since the life of an unborn child is precious in God's eyes.
  —Exodus 21:22, 23; Psalm 127:3.

- We show respect for life by not endangering it and by not eating blood.
  —Deuteronomy 5:17; Acts 15:28, 29.

---

# CHAPTER FOURTEEN

# How to Make Your Family Life Happy

**What is needed to be a good husband?**

**How can a woman succeed as a wife?**

**What is involved in being a fine parent?**

**How can children help to make family life happy?**

JEHOVAH GOD wants your family life to be happy. His Word, the Bible, provides guidelines for each family member, describing the role that God wants each one to play. When family members fulfill their roles in harmony with God's counsel, the results are very satisfying. Jesus said: "Happy are those hearing the word of God and keeping it!" —Luke 11:28.

² Family happiness depends mainly on our recognizing that the family originates with Jehovah, the one Jesus called "Our Father." (Matthew 6:9) Every

1. **What is the key to a happy family life?**
2. **Family happiness depends on our recognizing what?**

*What Does the Bible Really Teach?*

family on earth exists because of our heavenly Father—and he certainly knows what makes families happy. (Ephesians 3:14, 15) So, what does the Bible teach about the role of each family member?

## DIVINE ORIGIN OF HUMAN FAMILY

3 Jehovah created the first humans, Adam and Eve, and brought them together as husband and wife. He put them in a beautiful earthly paradise home—the garden of Eden—and told them to have children. "Be fruitful and become many and fill the earth," said Jehovah. (Genesis 1:26-28; 2:18, 21-24) This is not just a story or a myth, for Jesus showed that what Genesis says about the start of family life is true. (Matthew 19:4, 5) Although we face many problems and life now is not as God purposed it to be, let us see why happiness within the family is possible.

4 Each member of the family can help to make family life happy by imitating God in showing love.

3. How does the Bible describe the start of the human family, and why do we know that what it says is true?
4. (a) How can each member of the family contribute to its happiness? (b) Why is studying the life of Jesus so important to family happiness?

(Ephesians 5:1, 2) How, though, can we imitate God, since we cannot even see him? We can learn how Jehovah acts because he sent his firstborn Son from heaven to the earth. (John 1:14, 18) When on earth, this Son, Jesus Christ, imitated his heavenly Father so well that seeing and listening to Jesus was just like being with Jehovah and hearing Him. (John 14:9) Therefore, by learning about the love that Jesus showed and following his example, each one of us can help to make family life happier.

## A MODEL FOR HUSBANDS

5 The Bible says that husbands should treat their wives in the same way that Jesus treats his disciples. Consider this Bible direction: "Husbands, continue loving your wives, *just as the Christ also loved the congregation and delivered up himself for it* . . . In this way husbands ought to be loving their wives as their own bodies. He who loves his wife loves himself, for no man ever hated his own flesh; but he feeds and cherishes it, *as the Christ also does the congregation.*"—Ephesians 5:23, 25-29.

5, 6. (a) How does the way Jesus treats the congregation set an example for husbands? (b) What must be done to get forgiveness of sins?

*What Does the Bible Really Teach?*

⁶ Jesus' love for his congregation of disciples sets a perfect example for husbands. Jesus "loved them to the end," sacrificing his life for them, even though they were far from perfect. (John 13:1; 15:13) Similarly, husbands are urged: *"Keep on loving your wives and do not be bitterly angry with them."* (Colossians 3:19) What will help a husband to apply such counsel, especially if his wife at times fails to act with discretion? He should remember his own mistakes and what he must do to receive God's forgiveness. What is that? He must forgive those who sin against him, and that includes his wife. Of course, she should do the same. (Matthew 6:12, 14, 15) Do you see why some have said that a successful marriage is the union of two good forgivers?

⁷ Husbands also do well to note that Jesus always showed consideration for his disciples. He took into account their limitations and physical needs. When they were tired, for example, he said: "Come,

7. **What did Jesus take into account, setting what example for husbands?**

you yourselves, privately into a lonely place and rest up a bit." (Mark 6:30-32) Wives too deserve thoughtful consideration. The Bible describes them as "a weaker vessel" to whom husbands are commanded to assign "honor." Why? Because both husbands and wives share equally in "the undeserved favor of life." (1 Peter 3:7) Husbands should remember that it is faithfulness, not whether a person is male or female, that makes one precious to God.—Psalm 101:6.

⁸ The Bible says that a husband "who loves his wife loves himself." This is because a man and his wife "are no longer two, but *one flesh,*" as Jesus pointed out. (Matthew 19:6) So they must limit their sexual interests to each other. (Proverbs 5:15-21; Hebrews 13:4) They can do this if they show unselfish concern for each other's needs. (1 Corinthians 7:3-5) Noteworthy is the reminder: "No man ever hated his *own flesh; but he feeds and cherishes it.*" Husbands need to love their wives as they do

8. (a) How is it that a husband "who loves his wife loves himself"? (b) Being "one flesh" means what for a husband and his wife?

　　　　　　*What Does the Bible Really Teach?*

themselves, remembering that they are accountable to their own head, Jesus Christ.—Ephesians 5:29; 1 Corinthians 11:3.

⁹ The apostle Paul spoke of the 'tender affection that Christ Jesus has.' (Philippians 1:8) Jesus' tenderness was a refreshing quality, one that was appealing to women who became his disciples. (John 20:1, 11-13, 16) And wives yearn for tender affection from their husbands.

## AN EXAMPLE FOR WIVES

¹⁰ A family is an organization, and to operate smoothly, it needs a head. Even Jesus has One he submits to as his Head. "The head of the Christ is God," just as "the head of a woman is the man." (1 Corinthians 11:3) Jesus' submission to God's headship is a fine example, since all of us have a head to whom we must submit.

¹¹ Imperfect men make mistakes and often fall far short of being ideal family heads. So, what

9. What quality of Jesus is mentioned at Philippians 1:8, and why should husbands display this quality toward their wives?
10. How does Jesus provide an example for wives?
11. What attitude is a wife to have toward her husband, and what may be the effect of her conduct?

should a wife do? She should not belittle what her husband does or try to take over his headship. A wife does well to remember that in God's view, a quiet and mild spirit is of great value. (1 Peter 3:4) By displaying such a spirit, she will find it easier to demonstrate godly subjection, even under trying circumstances. Furthermore, the Bible says: "The wife should have deep respect for her husband." (Ephesians 5:33) But what if he does not accept Christ as his Head? The Bible urges wives: "Be in subjection to your own husbands, in order that, if any are not obedient to the word, they may be won without a word through the conduct of their wives, because of having been eyewitnesses of your chaste conduct together with *deep respect.*"—1 Peter 3:1, 2.

¹² Whether her husband is a fellow believer or not, a wife is not showing disrespect if she tactfully expresses an opinion that differs from his. Her viewpoint may be correct, and the whole family could benefit if he listened to her. Although Abraham did not agree when his wife, Sarah, recom-

**12. Why is it not wrong for a wife to express her opinions respectfully?**

*What Does the Bible Really Teach?*

mended a practical solution to a certain house-hold problem, God told him: "Listen to her voice." (Genesis 21:9-12) Of course, when a husband makes a final decision that does not conflict with God's law, his wife shows her subjection by supporting it. —Acts 5:29; Ephesians 5:24.

¹³ In fulfilling her role, a wife can do much in caring for the family. For example, the Bible shows that married women are "to love their husbands, to love their children, to be sound in mind, chaste, workers at home, good, subjecting themselves to their own husbands." (Titus 2:4, 5) A wife and mother who acts in this way will gain the lasting love and respect of her family. (Proverbs 31:10, 28) Since marriage is a union of imperfect individuals, however, some extreme circumstances may result in separation or divorce. The Bible allows for separation under certain circumstances. Yet, separation must not be taken lightly, for the Bible counsels: "A wife should not depart from her husband; . . .

13. (a) What does Titus 2:4, 5 urge married women to do? (b) What does the Bible say about separation and divorce?

*How to Make Your Family Life Happy*

and a husband should not leave his wife." (1 Corinthians 7:10, 11) And only fornication by one of the marriage mates provides Scriptural grounds for divorce.—Matthew 19:9.

## A PERFECT EXAMPLE FOR PARENTS

¹⁴ Jesus set a perfect example for parents in the way he treated children. When others tried to prevent the little ones from approaching Jesus, he said: "Let the young children come to me; do not try to stop them." The Bible says that he then "took the children into his arms and began blessing them, laying his hands upon them." (Mark 10:13-16) Since Jesus took time for little ones, should you not do the same for your own sons and daughters? They need, not small bits of your time, but large amounts of it. You need to take time to teach them, for that is what Jehovah instructs parents to do.—Deuteronomy 6:4-9.

¹⁵ As this world becomes ever more wicked, children need parents who will protect them from

**14. How did Jesus treat children, and what do children need from parents?**
**15. What can parents do to protect their children?**

*What Does the Bible Really Teach?*

people who seek to harm them, such as sexual predators. Consider how Jesus protected his disciples, whom he affectionately called "little children." When he was arrested and would soon be killed, Jesus made a way for them to escape. (John 13:33; 18:7-9) As a parent, you need to be alert to the Devil's attempts to harm your little ones. You need to give them advance warning.* (1 Peter 5:8) Never before has the threat to their physical, spiritual, and moral safety been greater.

16 On the night before Jesus died, his disciples argued about who was greater among them. Rather than become angry with them, Jesus lovingly continued to appeal to them by word and example. (Luke 22:24-27; John 13:3-8) If you are a parent, can you see how you might follow Jesus' example in the way you correct your children? True, they need discipline, but it should be given to "the proper degree" and never in anger. You would not

* Help in protecting children is found in chapter 32 of the book *Learn From the Great Teacher,* published by Jehovah's Witnesses.

**16. What can parents learn from the way that Jesus handled his disciples' imperfections?**

*Feb 12 '9 11*

*How to Make Your Family Life Happy*

*Deut 6 49*
*Jer 30 11*

want to speak thoughtlessly "as with the stabs of a sword." (Jeremiah 30:11; Proverbs 12:18) Discipline should be delivered in such a way that your child will later see how appropriate it was.—Ephesians 6:4; Hebrews 12:9-11.

## A MODEL FOR CHILDREN

17 Can children learn from Jesus? Yes, they can! By his own example, Jesus showed how children should obey their parents. "Just as the Father taught me," he said, "I speak." He added: "I always do the things pleasing to him." (John 8:28, 29) Jesus was obedient to his heavenly Father, and the Bible tells children to obey their parents. (Ephesians 6:1-3) Although Jesus was a perfect child, he obeyed his human parents, Joseph and Mary, who were imperfect. That surely contributed to the happiness of every member of Jesus' family!—Luke 2:4, 5, 51, 52.

18 Can children see ways that they can be more like Jesus and make their parents happy? True,

17. In what ways did Jesus set a perfect example for children?
18. Why did Jesus always obey his heavenly Father, and who is happy when children obey their parents today?

*What Does the Bible Really Teach?*

young ones may sometimes find it hard to obey their parents, but that is what God wants children to do. (Proverbs 1:8; 6:20) Jesus always obeyed his heavenly Father, even under difficult circumstances. Once, when it was God's will that Jesus do something especially hard, Jesus said: "Remove this cup [a certain requirement] from me." Nevertheless, Jesus did what God asked, because he realized that his Father knew best. (Luke 22:42) **By learning to be obedient, children will make their parents and their heavenly Father very happy.**\*—Proverbs 23:22-25.

¹⁹ The Devil tempted Jesus, and we can be sure that he will also tempt young ones to do what is wrong. (Matthew 4:1-10) Satan the Devil uses peer pressure, which can be hard to resist. How vital it is, then, that children not keep company with wrongdoers! (1 Corinthians 15:33) Jacob's daughter Dinah kept company with those who did not

------

\* Only if a parent asked a child to break God's law would it be right for the child to disobey.—Acts 5:29.

------

**19. (a) How does Satan tempt children? (b) What effect can the bad behavior of children have upon parents?**

worship Jehovah, and this led to a lot of trouble. (Genesis 34:1, 2) Think of how the family could be hurt if one of its members were to become involved in sexual immorality!—Proverbs 17:21, 25.

## THE KEY TO FAMILY HAPPINESS

[20] Family problems are easier to cope with when Bible counsel is applied. In fact, applying such counsel is the key to family happiness. So husbands, love your wife, and treat her as Jesus treats his congregation. Wives, submit to the headship of your husband, and follow the example of the capable wife described at Proverbs 31:10-31. Parents, train your children. (Proverbs 22:6) Fathers, 'preside over your household in a fine manner.' (1 Timothy 3:4, 5; 5:8) And children, obey your parents. (Colossians 3:20) None in the family are perfect, for all make mistakes. So be humble, asking one another for forgiveness.

[21] Truly, the Bible contains a wealth of valuable counsel and instruction regarding family life.

**20.** To enjoy happy family life, what must each family member do?
**21.** What wonderful prospects lie ahead, and how can we enjoy happy family life now?

*What Does the Bible Really Teach?*

Moreover, it teaches us about God's new world and an earthly paradise filled with happy people who worship Jehovah. (Revelation 21:3, 4) What wonderful prospects lie ahead! Even now, we can enjoy happy family life by applying God's instructions found in his Word, the Bible.

---

## WHAT THE BIBLE TEACHES

- Husbands need to love their wives as their own bodies.—Ephesians 5:25-29.

- Wives should love their family and respect their husbands.—Titus 2:4, 5.

- Parents need to love, teach, and protect their children.—Deuteronomy 6:4-9.

- Children need to obey their parents. —Ephesians 6:1-3.

---

# CHAPTER FIFTEEN

# Worship That God Approves

**Are all religions pleasing to God?**

**How can we identify the true religion?**

**Who are God's true worshipers on earth today?**

JEHOVAH GOD deeply cares for us and wants us to benefit from his loving direction. If we worship him in the right way, we will be happy and will avoid many problems in life. We will also have his blessing and his help. (Isaiah 48:17) There are, however, hundreds of religions that claim to teach the truth about God. Yet, they differ greatly in their teachings about who God is and what he expects of us.

² How can you know the right way to worship Jehovah? You do not have to study and compare the teachings of all the many religions. You need only learn what the Bible *really* teaches about true worship. To illustrate: In many lands, there is a problem with

1. How will we benefit if we worship God in the right way?
2. How can we learn the right way to worship Jehovah, and what illustration helps us to understand this?

*What Does the Bible Really Teach?*

counterfeit money. If you were given the job of picking out such false money, how would you go about it? By memorizing every kind of counterfeit? No. Your time would be better spent if you studied *real* money. After you knew what real money looked like, you could recognize a counterfeit. Similarly, when we learn how to identify the true religion, we can recognize those religions that are false.

³ It is important that we worship Jehovah in the way that he approves. Many people believe that all religions are pleasing to God, but the Bible does not teach that. It is not even enough just to claim to be a Christian. Jesus said: "Not everyone saying to me, 'Lord, Lord,' will enter into the kingdom of the heavens, but the one doing the will of my Father who is in the heavens will." To have God's approval, therefore, we must learn what God requires of us and do it. Jesus called those who do not do God's will "workers of lawlessness." (Matthew 7:21-23) Like counterfeit money, false religion has no real value. Even worse, such religion is actually harmful.

**3. According to Jesus, what must we do if we want to have God's approval?**

⁴ Jehovah gives everyone on earth the opportunity to gain everlasting life. To have eternal life in Paradise, however, we must worship God properly and live now in a way that is acceptable to him. Sadly, many refuse to do so. That is why Jesus said: "Go in through the narrow gate; because broad and spacious is the road leading off into destruction, and many are the ones going in through it; whereas narrow is the gate and cramped the road leading off into life, and few are the ones finding it." (Matthew 7:13, 14) True religion leads to everlasting life. False religion leads to destruction. Jehovah does not want any human to be destroyed, and that is why he is giving people everywhere an opportunity to learn about him. (2 Peter 3:9) Really, then, the way we worship God means either life or death for us.

## HOW TO IDENTIFY THE TRUE RELIGION

⁵ How can 'the road to life' be found? Jesus said that the true religion would be evident in the lives of the people who practice it. "By their fruits you will rec-

4. **What do Jesus' words concerning the two roads mean, and where does each road lead?**

5. **How can we recognize those who practice the true religion?**

*What Does the Bible Really Teach?*

ognize them," he said. "Every good tree produces fine fruit." (Matthew 7:16, 17) In other words, those who practice the true religion would be recognized by their beliefs and their conduct. Although they are not perfect and they make mistakes, true worshipers as a group seek to do God's will. Let us consider six features that identify those who practice true religion.

⁶ *God's servants base their teachings on the Bible.* The Bible itself says: "All Scripture is inspired of God and beneficial for teaching, for reproving, for setting things straight, for disciplining in righteousness, that the man [or woman] of God may be fully competent, completely equipped for every good work." (2 Timothy 3:16, 17) To his fellow Christians, the apostle Paul wrote: "When you received God's word, which you heard from us, you accepted it, not as the word of men, but, just as it truthfully is, as the word of God." (1 Thessalonians 2:13) Hence, beliefs and practices of the true religion are not based on human views or tradition. They originate in God's inspired Word, the Bible.

6, 7. How do God's servants view the Bible, and how did Jesus set the example in this regard?

## THOSE WHO WORSHIP THE TRUE GOD

- base their teachings on the Bible
- worship only Jehovah and make his name known
- show genuine love for one another
- accept Jesus as God's means of salvation
- are no part of the world
- preach God's Kingdom as man's only hope

[7] Jesus Christ set the proper example by basing his teachings on God's Word. In prayer to his heavenly Father, he said: "Your word is truth." (John 17:17) Jesus believed the Word of God, and everything he taught harmonized with the Scriptures. Jesus often said: "It is written." (Matthew 4:4, 7, 10) Then Jesus would quote a scripture. Similarly, God's people today do not teach their own ideas. They believe that the Bible is God's Word, and they base their teachings firmly on what it says.

[8] *Those who practice the true religion worship only Jehovah and make his name known.* Jesus declared: "It is Jehovah your God you must worship, and it is to him

8. **What is involved in worshiping Jehovah?**

*What Does the Bible Really Teach?*

alone you must render sacred service." (Matthew 4: 10) Thus, God's servants worship no one other than Jehovah. This worship includes letting people know what the name of the true God is and what he is like. Psalm 83:18 states: "You, whose name is Jehovah, you alone are the Most High over all the earth." Jesus set the pattern in helping others to get to know God, as he said in prayer: "I have made your name manifest to the men you gave me out of the world." (John 17:6) Similarly, true worshipers today teach others about God's name, his purposes, and his qualities.

9 *God's people show genuine, unselfish love for one another.* Jesus said: "By this all will know that you are my disciples, if you have love among yourselves." (John 13:35) The early Christians had such love for one another. Godly love overcomes racial, social, and national barriers and draws people together in an unbreakable bond of true brotherhood. (Colossians 3: 14) Members of false religions do not have such a loving brotherhood. How do we know that? They kill one another because of national or ethnic differences. True Christians do not take up weapons to kill their

9, 10. **In what ways do true Christians show love for one another?**

*Worship That God Approves*

Christian brothers or anyone else. The Bible states: "The children of God and the children of the Devil are evident by this fact: Everyone who does not carry on righteousness does not originate with God, neither does he who does not love his brother. . . . We should have love for one another; not like Cain, who originated with the wicked one and slaughtered his brother."—1 John 3:10-12; 4:20, 21.

¹⁰ Of course, genuine love means more than not killing others. True Christians unselfishly use their time, energy, and resources to help and encourage one another. (Hebrews 10:24, 25) They help one another in times of distress, and they deal honestly with others. In fact, they apply in their lives the Bible counsel to "work what is good toward all."—Galatians 6:10.

¹¹ *True Christians accept Jesus Christ as God's means of salvation.* The Bible says: "There is no salvation in anyone else, for there is not another name under heaven that has been given among men by which we must get saved." (Acts 4:12) As we saw in Chapter 5, Jesus gave his life as a ransom for obedient humans.

11. Why is it important to accept Jesus Christ as God's means of salvation?

*What Does the Bible Really Teach?*

(Matthew 20:28) In addition, Jesus is God's appointed King in the heavenly Kingdom that will rule the entire earth. And God requires that we obey Jesus and apply his teachings if we want everlasting life. That is why the Bible states: "He that exercises faith in the Son has everlasting life; he that disobeys the Son will not see life."—John 3:36.

¹² *True worshipers are no part of the world.* When on trial before the Roman ruler Pilate, Jesus said: "My kingdom is no part of this world." (John 18:36) No matter what country they live in, Jesus' true followers are subjects of his heavenly Kingdom and thus maintain strict neutrality in the world's political affairs. They take no part in its conflicts. However, Jehovah's worshipers do not interfere with what others choose to do about joining a political party, running for office, or voting. And while God's true worshipers are neutral regarding politics, they are law-abiding. Why? Because God's Word commands them to "be in subjection" to the governmental "superior authorities." (Romans 13:1) Where there is a conflict between what God requires and what a political system requires,

12. What does being no part of the world involve?

true worshipers follow the example of the apostles, who said: "We must obey God as ruler rather than men."—Acts 5:29; Mark 12:17.

¹³ *Jesus' true followers preach that God's Kingdom is mankind's only hope.* Jesus foretold: "This good news of the kingdom will be preached in all the inhabited earth for a witness to all the nations; and then the end will come." (Matthew 24:14) Instead of encouraging people to look to human rulers to solve their problems, true followers of Jesus Christ proclaim God's heavenly Kingdom as the only hope for mankind. (Psalm 146:3) Jesus taught us to pray for that perfect government when he said: "Let your kingdom come. Let your will take place, as in heaven, also upon earth." (Matthew 6:10) God's Word foretold that this heavenly Kingdom "will crush and put an end to all these kingdoms [now existing], and it itself will stand to times indefinite."—Daniel 2:44.

¹⁴ On the basis of what we have just considered, ask yourself: 'What religious group bases all its teachings

**13. How do Jesus' true followers view God's Kingdom, and therefore, what action do they take?**
**14. What religious group do you believe meets the requirements for true worship?**

*What Does the Bible Really Teach?*

on the Bible and makes known Jehovah's name? What group practices godly love, exercises faith in Jesus, is no part of the world, and proclaims that God's Kingdom is the only real hope for mankind? Of all the religious groups on earth, which one meets all these requirements?' The facts clearly show that it is Jehovah's Witnesses.—Isaiah 43:10-12.

## WHAT WILL YOU DO?

¹⁵ Simply believing in God is not enough to please him. After all, the Bible says that even the demons believe that God exists. (James 2:19) Obviously, though, they do not do God's will and do not have his approval. To be approved by God, not only must we believe in his existence but we must also do his will. We must also break free from false religion and embrace true worship.

¹⁶ The apostle Paul showed that we must not take part in false worship. He wrote: "'Get out from among them, and separate yourselves,' says Jehovah, 'and quit touching the unclean thing'; 'and I will take you in.'" (2 Corinthians 6:17; Isaiah 52:11) True

15. **What does God require in addition to believing that he exists?**
16. **What should be done about taking part in false religion?**

Christians therefore avoid anything that is connected with false worship.

¹⁷ The Bible shows that all the many forms of false religion are part of "Babylon the Great."* (Revelation 17:5) That name calls to mind the ancient city of Babylon, where false religion started up after the Flood of Noah's day. Many teachings and practices now common in false religion originated long ago in Babylon. For example, the Babylonians worshiped trinities, or triads, of gods. Today, the central doctrine of many religions is the Trinity. But the Bible clearly teaches that there is only one true God, Jehovah, and that Jesus Christ is his Son. (John 17:3) The Babylonians also believed that humans have an immortal soul that survives the body after death and can suffer in a place of torment. Today, belief in the immortal soul or spirit that can suffer in hellfire is taught by most religions.

¹⁸ Since ancient Babylonian worship spread

* For more information about why Babylon the Great represents the world empire of false religion, see the Appendix, pages 281-3.

**17, 18. What is "Babylon the Great," and why is it urgent to "get out of her"?**

throughout the earth, modern Babylon the Great can properly be identified as the world empire of false religion. And God has foretold that this empire of false religion will come to a sudden end. (Revelation 18:8) Do you see why it is vital that you separate yourself from every part of Babylon the Great? Jehovah God wants you to "get out of her" quickly while there is still time.—Revelation 18:4.

¹⁹ As a result of your decision to quit practicing false religion, some may choose to stop associating with you. By serving Jehovah with his people, however, you will gain far more than you could ever lose. Like Jesus' early disciples who left other things to follow him, you will come to have many spiritual brothers and sisters. You will become part of a large worldwide family of millions of true Christians, who show you genuine love. And you will have the wonderful hope of everlasting life "in the coming system of things." (Mark 10:28-30) Perhaps in time, those who abandoned you because of your beliefs will look into what the Bible teaches and become worshipers of Jehovah.

**19. What will you gain by serving Jehovah?**

**20** The Bible teaches that God will soon bring an end to this wicked system of things and will replace it with a righteous new world under the rulership of his Kingdom. (2 Peter 3:9, 13) What a marvelous world that will be! And in that righteous new system, there will be only one religion, one true form of worship. Is it not the course of wisdom for you to take the necessary steps to come into association with true worshipers right now?

**20. What does the future hold for those who practice the true religion?**

---

## WHAT THE BIBLE TEACHES

- There is only one true religion.
  —Matthew 7:13, 14.

- True religion is identified by its teachings and practices.—Matthew 7:16, 17.

- Jehovah's Witnesses practice the worship that God approves.—Isaiah 43:10.

# CHAPTER SIXTEEN

# Take Your Stand for True Worship

**What does the Bible teach about
the use of images?**

**What view do Christians take of
religious holidays?**

**How can you explain your beliefs to
others without offending them?**

SUPPOSE you found out that your whole neighborhood has been contaminated. Someone has secretly been dumping poisonous waste in the area, and now the situation is life threatening. What would you do? No doubt, you would move away if you could. But after doing that, you would still face this serious question, 'Have I been poisoned?'

² A similar situation arises with regard to false religion. The Bible teaches that such worship is contaminated with unclean teachings and practices. (2 Corinthians 6:17) That is why it is important for you to get

---

**1, 2. What question must you ask yourself after leaving false religion, and why do you think this is important?**

out of "Babylon the Great," the world empire of false religion. (Revelation 18:2, 4) Have you done this? If so, you are to be commended. But more is involved than just separating yourself or resigning from a false religion. Afterward, you must ask yourself, 'Do any traces of false worship remain in me?' Consider some examples.

## IMAGES AND ANCESTOR WORSHIP

³ Some have had images or shrines in their home for years. Is that true of you? If so, you might feel that it is strange or wrong to pray to God without such a visible aid. You may even feel attached to some of these items. But God is the one who says how he should be worshiped, and the Bible teaches that he does not want us to use images. (Exodus 20:4, 5; Psalm 115:4-8; Isaiah 42:8; 1 John 5:21) So you can take a stand for *true* worship by destroying any items you own that are connected with *false* worship. By all means, come to view them as Jehovah does—as something "detestable."—Deuteronomy 27:15.

3. (a) What does the Bible say about the use of images, and why might God's view be difficult for some to accept? (b) What should you do with any items you own that are connected with false worship?

⁴ Ancestor worship also is common in many false religions. Before learning Bible truth, some believed that the dead are conscious in an invisible realm and that they can help or harm the living. Perhaps you used to go to great lengths to appease your dead ancestors. But as you learned in Chapter 6 of this book, the dead have no conscious existence anywhere. Thus, attempts to communicate with them are of no use. Any messages that seem to come from a dead loved one really originate with the demons. Therefore, Jehovah forbade the Israelites to try to talk with the dead or to participate in any other form of spiritism.—Deuteronomy 18:10-12.

⁵ If the use of images or the practice of ancestor worship was part of your former way of worship, what can you do? Read and ponder over Bible passages that show you how God views these things. Pray to Jehovah daily about your desire to take a stand for true worship, and ask him to help you to think as he does.—Isaiah 55:9.

---

**4. (a) How do we know that ancestor worship is futile? (b) Why did Jehovah forbid his people to engage in any form of spiritism?**
**5. What can you do if the use of images or the practice of ancestor worship was in your religious past?**

# CHRISTMAS—NOT CELEBRATED BY EARLY CHRISTIANS

**6** A person's worship could be contaminated by false religion as it relates to popular holidays. Consider Christmas, for example. Christmas supposedly commemorates the birth of Jesus Christ, and nearly every religion that claims to be Christian celebrates it. Yet, there is no evidence that the first-century disciples of Jesus observed such a holiday. The book *Sacred Origins of Profound Things* states: "For two centuries after Christ's birth, no one knew, and few people cared, exactly when he was born."

**7** Even if Jesus' disciples had known the exact date of his birth, they would not have celebrated it. Why? Because, as *The World Book Encyclopedia* says, the early Christians "considered the celebration of anyone's birth to be a pagan custom." The only birthday observances mentioned in the Bible are those of two rulers who did not worship Jehovah. (Genesis 40:20; Mark 6:21) Birthday celebrations were also held in honor of pagan deities. For example, on May 24 the

**6, 7. (a) Christmas supposedly commemorates what, and did Jesus' first-century followers observe it? (b) What were birthday celebrations associated with during the time of Jesus' early disciples?**

*What Does the Bible Really Teach?*

Romans celebrated the birthday of the goddess Diana. On the following day, they observed the birthday of their sun-god, Apollo. Hence, birthday celebrations were associated with paganism, not with Christianity.

8 There is another reason why first-century Christians would not have celebrated Jesus' birthday. His disciples likely knew that birthday celebrations were connected with superstition. For instance, many Greeks and Romans of ancient times believed that a spirit attended the birth of each human and protected that one throughout life. "This spirit had a mystic relation with the god on whose birthday the individual was born," says the book *The Lore of Birthdays*. Jehovah certainly would not be pleased with any observance that would link Jesus with superstition. (Isaiah 65:11, 12) So how did Christmas come to be celebrated by many people?

## THE ORIGIN OF CHRISTMAS

9 It was not until several hundred years after Jesus lived on the earth that people began to commemorate

8. Explain the connection between birthday celebrations and superstition.
9. How did December 25 come to be regarded as the day to celebrate Jesus' birth?

his birth on December 25. But that was *not* the date of Jesus' birth, for it evidently took place in October.* So why was December 25 chosen? Some who later claimed to be Christian likely "wished the date to coincide with the pagan Roman festival marking the 'birthday of the unconquered sun.'" (*The New Encyclopædia Britannica*) In winter, when the sun seemed weakest, pagans held ceremonies to get this source of warmth and light to come back from its distant travels. December 25 was thought to be the day that the sun began its return. In an effort to convert pagans, religious leaders adopted this festival and tried to make it seem "Christian."#

¹⁰ The pagan roots of Christmas have long been recognized. Because of its unscriptural origin, Christmas was banned in England and in some of the American colonies during the 17th century. Anyone who even stayed home from work on Christmas day had to pay a penalty. Soon, though, the old customs

---

* See the Appendix, pages 283-5.

# The Saturnalia also played a part in the choice of December 25. This festival honoring the Roman god of agriculture took place on December 17-24. Feasting, merrymaking, and gift-giving took place during the Saturnalia.

**10. In times past, why did some people not celebrate Christmas?**

*What Does the Bible Really Teach?*

were back, and some new ones were added. Christmas once again became a big holiday, and that is what it still is in many lands. Because of the connections that Christmas has with false religion, however, those who want to please God do not celebrate it or any other holiday that has its roots in pagan worship.*

## DO ORIGINS REALLY MATTER?

[11] Some agree that such holidays as Christmas have pagan origins but still feel that it is not wrong to celebrate them. After all, most people are not thinking about false worship when they observe holidays. These occasions also give families opportunities to draw close together. Is this how you feel? If so, likely it is love of family, not love of false religion, that makes taking a stand for true worship seem difficult. Be assured that Jehovah, the one who originated the family, wants you to have a good relationship with your relatives. (Ephesians 3:14, 15) But you can strengthen such bonds in ways that God approves. Regarding the matter that should be our chief concern,

* For a discussion of how true Christians view other popular holidays, see the Appendix, pages 285-7.

**11. Why do some people celebrate holidays, but what should be our chief concern?**

the apostle Paul wrote: "Keep on making sure of what is acceptable to the Lord."—Ephesians 5:10.

12 Maybe you feel that the origins of holidays have little to do with how they are celebrated today. Do origins really matter? Yes! To illustrate: Suppose you saw a piece of candy lying in the gutter. Would you pick up that candy and eat it? Of course not! That candy is unclean. Like that candy, holidays may seem sweet, but they have been picked up from unclean places. To take a stand for true worship, we need to have a viewpoint like that of the prophet Isaiah, who told true worshipers: "Touch nothing unclean."—Isaiah 52:11.

## DISCERNMENT IN DEALING WITH OTHERS

13 Challenges may arise when you choose not to participate in holidays. For example, fellow employees may wonder why you do not engage in certain holiday activities where you work. What if you are offered a Christmas gift? Would it be wrong to accept it? What if your marriage mate does not share your be-

12. Illustrate why we should avoid customs and celebrations that have bad origins.
13. What challenges may arise when you do not participate in holidays?

liefs? How can you make sure that your children do not feel deprived because of not celebrating holidays?

14 Good judgment is needed to discern how to handle each situation. If a holiday greeting is casually extended, you could simply thank the well-wisher. But suppose you are dealing with someone you see or work with regularly. In that case, you might choose to say more. In all cases, be tactful. The Bible advises: "Let your utterance be always with graciousness, seasoned with salt, so as to know how you ought to give an answer to each one." (Colossians 4:6) Be careful not to show disrespect for others. Instead, tactfully explain your position. Make clear that you are not against gift-giving and gatherings but prefer to participate in these activities at a different time.

15 What if someone wants to give you a gift? Much depends upon the circumstances. The giver might say: "I know that you do not celebrate the holiday. Still, I want you to have this." You may decide that accepting the gift under those circumstances is not the same as taking part in the holiday. Of course, if the giver is not familiar with your beliefs, you could

14, 15. **What could you do if a holiday greeting is extended to you or if someone wants to give you a gift?**

mention that you do not observe the holiday. This would help to explain why you accept a gift but do not give one on that occasion. On the other hand, it would be wise not to accept a gift if it is given with the clear intention of showing that you do not stick to your beliefs or that you would compromise for the sake of material gain.

## WHAT ABOUT FAMILY MEMBERS?

16 What if family members do not share your beliefs? Again, be tactful. There is no need to make an issue of every custom or celebration that your relatives choose to observe. Instead, respect their right to their views, just as you want them to respect your right to yours. (Matthew 7:12) Avoid any actions that would make you a participant in the holiday. Still, be reasonable when it comes to matters that do not amount to actual celebration. Of course, you should always act in a way that will leave you with a good conscience.—1 Timothy 1:18, 19.

17 What can you do so that your children do not feel

16. How can you be tactful when handling matters related to holidays?
17. How can you help your children not to feel deprived because they see that others are celebrating holidays?

*What Does the Bible Really Teach?*

deprived because of not celebrating unscriptural holidays? Much depends on what you do at other times of the year. Some parents set aside times to give presents to their children. One of the best gifts you can give your children is your time and loving attention.

## PRACTICE TRUE WORSHIP

¹⁸ To please God, you must reject false worship and take a stand for true worship. What does this include? The Bible states: "Let us consider one another to incite to love and fine works, not forsaking the gathering of ourselves together, as some have the custom, but encouraging one another, and all the more so as you behold the day drawing near." (Hebrews 10:24, 25) Christian meetings are happy occasions for you to worship God in the way that he approves. (Psalm 22:22; 122:1) At such meetings, there is "an interchange of encouragement" among faithful Christians. —Romans 1:12.

¹⁹ Another way that you can take a stand for true worship is to speak to others about the things you

**18.** How can attending Christian meetings help you to take a stand for true worship?
**19.** Why is it important that you speak to others about the things you have learned from the Bible?

have learned from studying the Bible with Jehovah's Witnesses. Many people truly are "sighing and groaning" over the wickedness that is taking place in the world today. (Ezekiel 9:4) Perhaps you know some people who feel that way. Why not speak to them about your Bible-based hope for the future? As you associate with true Christians and speak to others about the marvelous Bible truths you have learned, you will find that any desire for the customs of false worship that may have remained in your heart will gradually disappear. Be assured that you will be very happy and will receive many blessings if you take your stand for true worship.—Malachi 3:10.

---

## WHAT THE BIBLE TEACHES

- Neither images nor ancestor worship have any place in true worship.—Exodus 20:4, 5; Deuteronomy 18:10-12.

- It is wrong to take part in celebrations that have pagan origins.—Ephesians 5:10.

- True Christians should be tactful when they explain their beliefs to others. —Colossians 4:6.

---

*What Does the Bible Really Teach?*

# CHAPTER SEVENTEEN

# Draw Close to God in Prayer

**Why should we pray to God?** *He invites*

**What must we do to be heard by God?** *faith*

*in accord wi Jehovah in Jesus name*

**How does God answer our prayers?**

COMPARED with the vast universe, the earth is very small. In fact, to Jehovah, "the Maker of heaven and earth," the nations of mankind are like a tiny drop of water from a bucket. (Psalm 115:15; Isaiah 40:15) Yet, the Bible says: "Jehovah is near to all those calling upon him, to all those who call upon him in trueness. The desire of those fearing him he will perform, and their cry for help he will hear." (Psalm 145:18, 19) Just think of what that means! The almighty Creator is near to us and will hear us if we "call upon him in trueness." What a privilege we have to approach God in prayer!

² If we want Jehovah to listen to our prayers,

---

**1, 2. Why should we view prayer as a great privilege, and why do we need to know what the Bible teaches about it?**

however, we must pray to him in the way that he approves. How can we do this unless we understand what the Bible teaches about prayer? It is vital for us to know what the Scriptures say on this subject, for prayer helps us to draw closer to Jehovah.

## WHY PRAY TO JEHOVAH?

³ One important reason why we should pray to Jehovah is that he invites us to do so. His Word encourages us: "Do not be anxious over anything, but in everything by prayer and supplication along with thanksgiving let your petitions be made known to God; and the peace of God that excels all thought will guard your hearts and your mental powers by means of Christ Jesus." (Philippians 4:6, 7) Surely we would not want to ignore such a kind provision made for us by the Supreme Ruler of the universe!

⁴ Another reason to pray is that regularly praying to Jehovah is a way to strengthen our relationship with him. True friends do not commu-

3. What is one important reason why we should pray to Jehovah?
4. How does regular prayer to Jehovah strengthen our relationship with him?

*What Does the Bible Really Teach?*

nicate only when they need something. Rather, good friends are interested in each other, and their friendship becomes stronger as they freely express their thoughts, concerns, and feelings. In some respects, the situation is similar when it comes to our relationship with Jehovah God. With the help of this book, you have learned much about what the Bible teaches regarding Jehovah, his personality, and his purposes. You have come to know him as a real person. Prayer gives you the opportunity to express your thoughts and innermost feelings to your heavenly Father. As you do, you draw closer to Jehovah.—James 4:8.

## WHAT REQUIREMENTS MUST WE MEET?

⁵ Does Jehovah listen to all prayers? Consider what he told rebellious Israelites in the days of the prophet Isaiah: "Even though you make many prayers, I am not listening; with bloodshed your very hands have become filled." (Isaiah 1:15) So certain actions can cause God not to listen to our prayers. For our prayers to be favorably

5. What shows that Jehovah does not listen to all prayers?

heard by God, therefore, we must meet some basic requirements.

⁶ A primary requirement is that we exercise faith. (Mark 11:24) The apostle Paul wrote: "Without faith it is impossible to please [God] well, for he that approaches God must believe that he is and that he becomes the rewarder of those earnestly seeking him." (Hebrews 11:6) Having true faith is more than merely knowing that God exists and that he hears and answers prayers. Faith is proved by our actions. We must give clear evidence that we have faith by the way we live every day.—James 2:26.

⁷ Jehovah also requires that those who approach him in prayer do so with humility and sincerity. Do we not have reason to be humble when speaking to Jehovah? When people have the opportunity to speak to a king or a president, they usually do so respectfully, acknowledging the ruler's high po-

6. In order for God to listen to our prayers, what is a primary requirement, and how can we meet it?
7. (a) Why should we be respectful when speaking to Jehovah in prayer? (b) When praying to God, how can we show humility and sincerity?

*What Does the Bible Really Teach?*

sition. How much more so should we be respectful when approaching Jehovah! (Psalm 138:6) After all, he is "God Almighty." (Genesis 17:1) When we pray to God, the manner in which we approach him should show that we humbly recognize our position before him. Such humility will also move us to pray from our heart in sincerity, avoiding routine, repetitive prayers.—Matthew 6:7, 8.

⁸ Another requirement for being heard by God is that we act in harmony with our prayers. Jehovah expects us to do all that is within our power to work at what we pray for. For example, if we pray, "Give us today our bread for this day," we must work hard at whatever available job we are able to perform. (Matthew 6:11; 2 Thessalonians 3:10) If we pray for help in overcoming a fleshly weakness, we must be careful to avoid circumstances and situations that could lead us into temptation. (Colossians 3:5) In addition to these basic requirements, there are questions about prayer that we need to have answered.

8. How can we act in harmony with what we pray for?

## ANSWERING SOME QUESTIONS
## ABOUT PRAYER

**9** *To whom should we pray?* Jesus taught his followers to pray to "our Father in the heavens." (Matthew 6:9) Our prayers, then, must be directed only to Jehovah God. However, Jehovah requires that we acknowledge the position of his only-begotten Son, Jesus Christ. As we learned in Chapter 5, Jesus was sent to the earth to serve as a ransom to redeem us from sin and death. (John 3:16; Romans 5:12) He is the appointed High Priest and Judge. (John 5:22; Hebrews 6:20) Hence, the Scriptures direct us to offer our prayers through Jesus. He himself said: "I am the way and the truth and the life. No one comes to the Father except through me." (John 14:6) For our prayers to be heard, we must pray only *to* Jehovah *through* his Son.

**10** *Must we assume a special position or posture when praying?* No. Jehovah does not require any specific position, either of the hands or of the whole body. The Bible teaches that it is acceptable to pray in a

9. To whom should we pray, and through whom?
10. Why is no specific position or posture required when we pray?

wide variety of positions. These include sitting, bowing, kneeling, and standing. (1 Chronicles 17: 16; Nehemiah 8:6; Daniel 6:10; Mark 11:25) What is truly important is, not some special posture that can be seen by others, but the right heart attitude. In fact, during our daily activities or when we are faced with an emergency, we may offer a silent prayer wherever we are. Jehovah hears such prayers even though they may go completely unnoticed by those around us.—Nehemiah 2:1-6.

11 *What may we pray for?* The Bible explains: "No matter what it is that we ask according to his will, he [Jehovah] hears us." (1 John 5:14) So we may pray for anything that is in harmony with God's will. Is it his will that we pray about personal concerns? By all means! Praying to Jehovah can be much like talking to a close friend. We may speak openly, 'pouring out our heart' to God. (Psalm 62:8) It is proper for us to ask for holy spirit, for it will help us to do what is right. (Luke 11:13) We can also ask for guidance in making wise decisions

11. **What are some personal concerns that are proper subjects of prayer?**

*Draw Close to God in Prayer*

and for strength in coping with difficulties. (James 1:5) When we sin, we should ask for forgiveness on the basis of Christ's sacrifice. (Ephesians 1:3, 7) Of course, personal matters should not be the only subjects of our prayers. We should broaden out our prayers to include other people—family members as well as fellow worshipers.—Acts 12:5; Colossians 4:12.

¹² Matters relating to Jehovah God should be given first importance in our prayers. We certainly have reason to express heartfelt praise and thanks to him for all his goodness. (1 Chronicles 29:10-13) Jesus gave the model prayer, recorded at Matthew 6:9-13, in which he taught us to pray that God's name be sanctified, that is, treated as sacred, or holy. That God's Kingdom come and that his will be done on the earth as it is in heaven are mentioned next. Only after covering these important matters relating to Jehovah did Jesus give attention to personal concerns. When we likewise give God

**12. How may we give matters concerning our heavenly Father first importance in our prayers?**

*What Does the Bible Really Teach?*

the most important place in our prayers, we show that we are interested in more than just our own welfare.

13 *How long should our prayers be?* The Bible does not place any limit on how long private or public prayers should be. They may range from a brief prayer before a meal to a long private prayer in which we pour out our heart to Jehovah. (1 Samuel 1:12, 15) However, Jesus condemned self-righteous individuals who made long, showy prayers before others. (Luke 20:46, 47) Such prayers do not impress Jehovah. What is important is that we pray from our heart. Hence, the length of acceptable prayers may vary according to needs and circumstances.

14 *How often should we pray?* The Bible encourages us to "pray continually," to "persevere in prayer," and to "pray incessantly." (Matthew 26:41; Romans 12:12; 1 Thessalonians 5:17) Of course, these

---

**13. What do the Scriptures indicate about the length of acceptable prayers?**

**14. What does the Bible mean when it encourages us to "pray continually," and what is comforting about this?**

statements do not mean that we must be praying to Jehovah every moment of the day. Rather, the Bible is urging us to pray regularly, continually thanking Jehovah for his goodness to us and looking to him for guidance, comfort, and strength. Is it not comforting to know that Jehovah puts no limit on how long or how often we can talk to him in prayer? If we truly appreciate the privilege of prayer, we will find many opportunities to pray to our heavenly Father.

¹⁵ *Why should we say "Amen" at the end of a prayer?* The word "amen" means "surely," or "so be it." Scriptural examples show that it is appropriate to say "Amen" at the close of personal and public prayers. (1 Chronicles 16:36; Psalm 41:13) By saying "Amen" at the end of our own prayer, we affirm that our expressions were made with sincerity. When we say "Amen"—either silently or out loud—at the end of someone's public prayer, we indicate that we are in agreement with the thoughts that were expressed.—1 Corinthians 14:16.

**15. Why should we say "Amen" at the end of personal and public prayers?**

*What Does the Bible Really Teach?*

# HOW GOD ANSWERS OUR PRAYERS

¹⁶ Does Jehovah really answer prayers? Yes, indeed! We have a firm basis to be confident that the "Hearer of prayer" answers sincere prayers offered by millions of humans. (Psalm 65:2) Jehovah's answer to our prayers may come in a variety of ways.

¹⁷ Jehovah uses his angels and his earthly servants to answer prayers. (Hebrews 1:13, 14) There have been many experiences of individuals who prayed to God for help to understand the Bible and were soon thereafter contacted by one of Jehovah's servants. Such experiences give evidence of angelic direction of the Kingdom-preaching work. (Revelation 14:6) To answer our prayers offered in a time of real need, Jehovah may motivate a Christian to come to our aid.—Proverbs 12:25; James 2:16.

¹⁸ Jehovah God also uses his holy spirit and his Word, the Bible, to answer the prayers of his servants. He may answer our prayers for help to cope

16. What confidence can we have regarding prayer?
17. Why can it be said that God uses his angels and his earthly servants to answer our prayers?
18. How does Jehovah use his holy spirit and his Word to answer the prayers of his servants?

*Draw Close to God in Prayer*

with trials by giving us guidance and strength by means of his holy spirit. (2 Corinthians 4:7) Often the answer to our prayers for direction comes from the Bible, where Jehovah gives us help in making wise decisions. Helpful scriptures may be found during our personal Bible study and as we read Christian publications, such as this book. Scriptural points that we need to consider may be brought to our attention by what is said at a Christian meeting or through the comments of a concerned elder in the congregation.—Galatians 6:1.

¹⁹ If Jehovah seems to delay in answering our prayers, this is never because he is not able to answer them. Rather, we must remember that Jehovah answers prayers according to his will and in his due time. He knows our needs and how to care for them far better than we do. Often he allows us to 'keep on asking, seeking, and knocking.' (Luke 11: 5-10) Such perseverance shows God that our desire is very deep and that our faith is genuine. Furthermore, Jehovah may answer our prayers in a way

**19. What should we keep in mind if our prayers sometimes seem to go unanswered?**

*What Does the Bible Really Teach?*

that is not obvious to us. For example, he may answer our prayer regarding a particular trial, not by removing the difficulty, but by giving us the strength to endure it.—Philippians 4:13.

20 How thankful we can be that the Creator of this vast universe is close to all who call upon him properly in prayer! (Psalm 145:18) May we take full advantage of the precious privilege of prayer. If we do, we will have the joyous prospect of drawing ever closer to Jehovah, the Hearer of prayer.

**20. Why should we take full advantage of the precious privilege of prayer?**

---

### WHAT THE BIBLE TEACHES

- Regularly praying to Jehovah helps us to draw closer to him.—James 4:8.

- For our prayers to be heard by God, we must pray in faith and with humility and sincerity.—Mark 11:24.

- We must pray only to Jehovah through his Son.—Matthew 6:9; John 14:6.

- Jehovah, the "Hearer of prayer," uses his angels, his earthly servants, his holy spirit, and his Word to answer prayers.—Psalm 65:2.

---

*Draw Close to God in Prayer*

# CHAPTER EIGHTEEN

# Baptism and Your Relationship With God

**How is Christian baptism performed?**

**What steps do you need to take to qualify for baptism?**

**How does a person make a dedication to God?**

**What is the special reason for getting baptized?**

"LOOK! A body of water; what prevents me from getting baptized?" That question was asked by an Ethiopian court official in the first century. A Christian named Philip had proved to him that Jesus was the promised Messiah. Touched to the heart by what he had learned from the Scriptures, the Ethiopian man took action. He showed that he wanted to be baptized!—Acts 8:26-36.

² If you have carefully studied the earlier chapters of this book with one of Jehovah's Witness-

**1. Why did an Ethiopian court official request baptism?**
**2. Why should you think seriously about baptism?**

es, you may feel ready to ask, 'What prevents *me* from getting baptized?' By now you have learned about the Bible's promise of everlasting life in Paradise. (Luke 23:43; Revelation 21:3, 4) You have also learned about the true condition of the dead and the resurrection hope. (Ecclesiastes 9:5; John 5:28, 29) You have probably been associating with Jehovah's Witnesses at their congregation meetings and have seen for yourself how they practice the true religion. (John 13:35) Most important, you have likely begun to develop a personal relationship with Jehovah God.

³ How can you show that you want to serve God? Jesus told his followers: "Go . . . and make disciples of people of all the nations, *baptizing them.*" (Matthew 28:19) Jesus himself set the example by being baptized in water. He was not sprinkled with water, and he did not just have some water poured over his head. (Matthew 3:16) The word "baptize" comes from a Greek term meaning "dip." Christian

3. (a) What command did Jesus give his followers? (b) How is water baptism performed?

baptism therefore means being fully dipped, or immersed, in water.

4 Water baptism is a requirement for all who want to have a relationship with Jehovah God. Baptism publicly indicates your desire to serve God. It shows that you are delighted to do Jehovah's will. (Psalm 40:7, 8) To qualify for baptism, however, you must take definite steps.

## KNOWLEDGE AND FAITH NEEDED

5 You have already begun to take the first step. How? By *taking in knowledge* of Jehovah God and Jesus Christ, perhaps by means of a systematic study of the Bible. (John 17:3) But there is more to learn. Christians want to be "filled with the accurate knowledge of [God's] will." (Colossians 1:9) Attending the congregation meetings of Jehovah's Witnesses is a big help in this regard. It is important to attend such meetings. (Hebrews 10:24, 25) Regular meeting attendance will help you increase your knowledge of God.

4. What does water baptism indicate?
5. (a) What is the first step in qualifying for baptism? (b) Why are Christian meetings important?

*What Does the Bible Really Teach?*

⁶ Of course, you do not need to know everything in the Bible in order to qualify for baptism. The Ethiopian court official had *some* knowledge, but he needed help to understand certain parts of the Scriptures. (Acts 8:30, 31) Likewise, you still have much to learn. In fact, you will never stop learning about God. (Ecclesiastes 3:11) Before you can be baptized, however, you need to know and accept at least the basic Bible teachings. (Hebrews 5:12) Such teachings include the truth about the condition of the dead and the importance of God's name and his Kingdom.

⁷ Knowledge alone is not enough, though, for "without faith it is impossible to please [God] well." (Hebrews 11:6) The Bible tells us that when some people in the ancient city of Corinth heard the Christian message, they "began to believe and be baptized." (Acts 18:8) In a similar way, a study of the Bible should fill you with *faith* that it is the inspired Word of God. Bible study should help you

6. How much Bible knowledge must you have in order to qualify for baptism?
7. What effect should a study of the Bible have on you?

to have faith in God's promises and in the saving power of Jesus' sacrifice.—Joshua 23:14; Acts 4:12; 2 Timothy 3:16, 17.

## SHARING BIBLE TRUTH WITH OTHERS

[8] As faith grows in your heart, you will find it hard to keep what you have learned to yourself. (Jeremiah 20:9) You will be strongly motivated to speak to others about God and his purposes. —2 Corinthians 4:13.

[9] You might begin to share Bible truth with others by tactfully speaking about it to your relatives, friends, neighbors, and workmates. In time, you will want to share in the organized preaching work of Jehovah's Witnesses. At that point, feel free to talk things over with the Witness who is teaching you the Bible. If it appears that you qualify for the public ministry, arrangements will be made for you and your teacher to meet with two of the congregation elders.

---

**8. What will move you to share with others what you have learned?**
**9, 10. (a) With whom might you begin sharing Bible truth? (b) What should you do if you want to share in the organized preaching work of Jehovah's Witnesses?**

*What Does the Bible Really Teach?*

**10** This will enable you to get better acquainted with some Christian elders, who shepherd the flock of God. (Acts 20:28; 1 Peter 5:2, 3) If these elders see that you understand and believe basic Bible teachings, are living in harmony with God's principles, and truly want to be one of Jehovah's Witnesses, they will let you know that you qualify to share in the public ministry as an unbaptized publisher of the good news.

**11** On the other hand, you may need to make some changes in your life-style and habits in order to qualify for the public ministry. This may include stopping some practices that have been kept secret from others. Hence, before you ask about becoming an unbaptized publisher, you need to be free of serious sins, such as sexual immorality, drunkenness, and drug abuse.—1 Corinthians 6:9, 10; Galatians 5:19-21.

## REPENTANCE AND CONVERSION

**12** Some other steps must be taken before you

11. What changes might some have to make before they qualify for the public ministry?
12. Why is repentance necessary?

*Baptism and Your Relationship With God*                                    227

qualify for baptism. The apostle Peter said: "Repent . . . and turn around so as to get your sins blotted out." (Acts 3:19) To repent is to feel sincere regret over something you have done. *Repentance* is clearly fitting if a person has lived an immoral life, but it is also necessary even if one has lived a relatively clean life morally. Why? Because all humans are sinners and need God's forgiveness. (Romans 3:23; 5:12) Before studying the Bible, you did not know what God's will was. So how could you have lived in full harmony with his will? Therefore, repentance is necessary.

[13] Repentance must be followed by *conversion,* or 'turning around.' You must do more than feel regret. You need to reject your former way of life and be firmly determined that you will do what is right from now on. Repentance and conversion are steps that you must take before being baptized.

## MAKING A PERSONAL DEDICATION

[14] There is another important step to take before

13. What is conversion?
14. What important step must you take before being baptized?

being baptized. You must *dedicate* yourself to Jehovah God.

¹⁵ When you dedicate yourself to Jehovah God in earnest prayer, you promise to give him your exclusive devotion forever. (Deuteronomy 6:15) Why, though, would someone want to do that? Well, suppose a man has begun to court a woman. The more he learns about her and sees that she has fine qualities, the more he finds himself drawn to her. In time, it is natural that he would ask her to marry him. True, getting married will mean taking on additional responsibilities. But love will move him to take that important step.

¹⁶ When you come to know and love Jehovah, you are moved to serve him without holding anything back or setting any limits in worshiping him. Anyone who wants to follow God's Son, Jesus Christ, has to "disown himself." (Mark 8:34) We disown ourselves by making sure that personal desires and goals do not stand in the way of our complete obedience to God. Before you can be baptized, then,

**15, 16. What does it mean to dedicate yourself to God, and what moves a person to do this?**

doing Jehovah God's will must be your main purpose in life.—1 Peter 4:2.

## OVERCOMING FEAR OF FAILURE

¹⁷ Some hold back from making a dedication to Jehovah because they are somewhat afraid of taking such a serious step. They may fear being accountable to God as a dedicated Christian. Being afraid that they may fail and disappoint Jehovah, they think that it is best not to make a dedication to him.

¹⁸ As you learn to love Jehovah, you will be moved to make a dedication to him and to do your best to live up to it. (Ecclesiastes 5:4) After making a dedication, surely you will want to "walk worthily of Jehovah to the end of fully pleasing him." (Colossians 1:10) Because of your love for God, you will not think it is too hard to do his will. No doubt you will agree with the apostle John, who wrote: "This is what the love of God means, that we observe his commandments; and yet his commandments are not burdensome."—1 John 5:3.

17. Why might some hold back from making a dedication to God?
18. What can move you to make a dedication to Jehovah?

**19** You do not have to be perfect to make a dedication to God. Jehovah knows your limitations and never expects you to do more than you are able to do. (Psalm 103:14) He wants you to succeed and will support and help you. (Isaiah 41:10) You can be sure that if you trust in Jehovah with all your heart, he "will make your paths straight."—Proverbs 3:5, 6.

## SYMBOLIZING YOUR DEDICATION BY GETTING BAPTIZED

**20** Thinking about the things we have just discussed may help you to make a personal dedication to Jehovah in prayer. Everyone who really loves God must also 'make public declaration for salvation.' (Romans 10:10) How do you go about doing that?

**21** Let the presiding overseer of your congregation know that you want to get baptized. He will arrange for some elders to review with you a number of questions that cover the Bible's basic teachings. If

19. Why do you not need to fear making a dedication to God?
20. Why can dedication to Jehovah not remain a private matter?
21, 22. How can you make "public declaration" of your faith?

these elders agree that you qualify, they will tell you that you can be baptized at the next opportunity.* A talk reviewing the meaning of baptism is usually given on such occasions. The speaker then invites all baptism candidates to answer two simple questions as one way to make a verbal "public declaration" of their faith.

²² It is the baptism itself that publicly identifies you as a person who has made a dedication to God and is now one of Jehovah's Witnesses. Baptism candidates are fully immersed in water to show publicly that they have made a dedication to Jehovah.

## THE MEANING OF YOUR BAPTISM

²³ Jesus said that his disciples would be baptized "in the name of the Father and of the Son and of the holy spirit." (Matthew 28:19) This means that a baptism candidate recognizes the authority of Jehovah God and of Jesus Christ. (Psalm 83:18; Mat-

_____

* Baptisms are a regular feature of annual assemblies and conventions held by Jehovah's Witnesses.

_____

**23. What does it mean to be baptized "in the name of the Father and of the Son and of the holy spirit"?**

*What Does the Bible Really Teach?*

thew 28:18) He also recognizes the function and activity of God's holy spirit, or active force.—Galatians 5:22, 23; 2 Peter 1:21.

24 However, baptism is not a mere bath. It is a symbol of something very important. Going beneath the water symbolizes that you have died to your former life course. Being raised up out of the water indicates that you are now alive to do the will of God. Remember, too, that you have made a dedication to Jehovah God himself, not to a work, a cause, other humans, or an organization. Your dedication and baptism are the beginning of a very close friendship with God—an intimate relationship with him.—Psalm 25:14.

25 Baptism does not guarantee salvation. The apostle Paul wrote: "Keep working out your own salvation with fear and trembling." (Philippians 2:12) Baptism is only a beginning. The question is, How can you remain in God's love? Our final chapter will provide the answer.

**24, 25. (a) What does baptism symbolize? (b) What question needs to be answered?**

# WHAT THE BIBLE TEACHES

- Christian baptism involves complete immersion in water, not just sprinkling. —Matthew 3:16.

- Steps leading to baptism begin with taking in knowledge and showing faith followed by repentance, conversion, and the dedicating of oneself to God.—John 17:3; Acts 3:19; 18:8.

- To make a dedication to Jehovah, you must disown yourself, even as people disowned themselves to follow Jesus.—Mark 8:34.

- Baptism symbolizes dying to one's former way of life and becoming alive to do God's will. —1 Peter 4:2.

*What Does the Bible Really Teach?*

# CHAPTER NINETEEN

# Remain in God's Love

**What does it mean to love God?**

**How can we remain in God's love?**

**How will Jehovah reward those who remain in his love?**

PICTURE yourself walking along a road on a stormy day. The sky becomes darker. Lightning starts to flash, thunder booms, then rain falls in torrents. You hurry along, desperately looking for a refuge. There, by the roadside, you see a shelter. It is sturdy, dry, and inviting. How you value that safe place!

² We are living in stormy times. World conditions are going from bad to worse. But there is a secure shelter, a refuge that can keep us safe from permanent harm. What is it? Note what the Bible teaches: "I will say to Jehovah: 'You are my refuge and my stronghold, my God, in whom I will trust.'"—Psalm 91:2.

³ Imagine that! Jehovah, the Creator and Sovereign

1, 2. Where can we find a safe refuge today?
3. How can we make Jehovah our refuge?

of the universe, can be our protective refuge. He can keep us safe, for he is far more powerful than anyone or anything that may come against us. Even if we are harmed, Jehovah can undo all the bad effects. How can we make Jehovah our refuge? We need to trust in him. Furthermore, God's Word urges us: "Keep yourselves in God's love." (Jude 21) Yes, we need to remain in God's love, maintaining a loving bond with our heavenly Father. Then we may rest assured that he is our refuge. But how can we form such a bond?

## RECOGNIZE AND RESPOND TO GOD'S LOVE

⁴ To remain in God's love, we need to appreciate how Jehovah has shown his love for us. Think of some of the Bible teachings you have learned with the aid of this book. As the Creator, Jehovah has given us the earth as our delightful home. He has filled it with abundant food and water, natural resources, fascinating animal life, and beautiful scenery. As the Author of the Bible, God has revealed his name and his qualities to us. Moreover, his Word reveals that he sent his own beloved Son to the earth, allowing Jesus to suffer

**4, 5. What are some of the ways that Jehovah has expressed love for us?**

*What Does the Bible Really Teach?*

and die for us. (John 3:16) And what does that gift mean for us? It gives us hope for a wonderful future.

⁵ Our hope for the future also depends on something else that God has done. Jehovah has established a heavenly government, the Messianic Kingdom. It will soon bring an end to all suffering and will make the earth a paradise. Just think! We can live there in peace and happiness forever. (Psalm 37:29) Meanwhile, God has given us guidance on how to live in the best way possible right now. He has also given us the gift of prayer, an open line of communication with him. These are just a few of the ways that Jehovah has shown love for mankind in general and for you as an individual.

⁶ The vital question for you to consider is this: How will I respond to Jehovah's love? Many will say, "Well, I need to love Jehovah in return." Is that how you feel? Jesus said that this command is the greatest of all: "You must love Jehovah your God with your whole heart and with your whole soul and with your whole mind." (Matthew 22:37) You certainly have many reasons to love Jehovah God. But is *feeling* that you have such love all that is involved in loving Jehovah with your whole heart, soul, and mind?

**6. How might you respond to the love that Jehovah has shown you?**

⁷ As described in the Bible, love for God is much more than a feeling. In fact, although the feeling of love for Jehovah is essential, that feeling is just the beginning of real love for him. An apple seed is essential to the development of a fruit-bearing apple tree. If you wanted an apple, however, would you be content if someone merely handed you an apple seed? Hardly! Similarly, a feeling of love for Jehovah God is only a start. The Bible teaches: "This is what the love of God means, that we observe his commandments; and yet his commandments are not burdensome." (1 John 5:3) To be genuine, love for God must bear fine fruit. It must be expressed in actions.—Matthew 7:16-20.

⁸ We show our love for God when we observe his commandments and apply his principles. It is not too hard to do so. Far from being burdensome, Jehovah's laws are designed to help us live a good, happy, satisfying life. (Isaiah 48:17, 18) By living in harmony with Jehovah's guidance, we show our heavenly Father that we truly appreciate all that he has done for us. Sadly, too few in today's world show such appreciation. We do not want to be unappreciative, like some people

---

7. Is there more to loving God than simply experiencing a feeling? Explain.
8, 9. How can we express our love and appreciation for God?

who lived when Jesus was on earth. Jesus healed ten lepers, but *only one* turned back to thank him. (Luke 17:12-17) Surely we would want to be like the grateful one, not the ungrateful nine!

⁹ What, then, are Jehovah's commandments that we need to observe? We have discussed a number of them in this book, but let us review a few. Observing God's commandments will help us to remain in God's love.

## DRAW EVER CLOSER TO JEHOVAH

¹⁰ Learning about Jehovah is a vital step in drawing closer to him. It is a process that should never stop. If you were outside on a very cold night warming yourself by a fire, would you let the flames dwindle and then die out? No. You would keep adding fuel to keep the fire burning bright and hot. Your very life might be at stake! As wood fuels a fire, so "the very knowledge of God" keeps our love for Jehovah strong.—Proverbs 2: 1-5.

¹¹ Jesus wanted his followers to keep their love for Jehovah and for His precious Word of truth alive and burning brightly. After his resurrection, Jesus taught

10. **Explain why it is important to continue taking in knowledge about Jehovah God.**
11. **What effect did Jesus' teaching have on his followers?**

two of his disciples about some of the prophecies in the Hebrew Scriptures that were fulfilled in him. What was the effect? They later said: "Were not our hearts burning as he was speaking to us on the road, as he was fully opening up the Scriptures to us?"—Luke 24:32.

¹² When you first learned what the Bible really teaches, did you find that your heart began to burn with joy, zeal, and love for God? No doubt you did. Many have felt the same way. The challenge now is to keep that intense love alive and to help it grow. We do not want to follow the trend of today's world. Jesus foretold: "The love of the greater number will cool off." (Matthew 24:12) How can you prevent your love for Jehovah and for Bible truths from cooling off?

¹³ Keep taking in knowledge of Jehovah God and Jesus Christ. (John 17:3) Meditate, or think deeply, on what you learn from God's Word, asking yourself: 'What does this teach me about Jehovah God? What further reason does it give me to love him with my whole heart, mind, and soul?' (1 Timothy 4:15) Such meditation will keep your love for Jehovah burning brightly.

12, 13. (a) Among the majority of mankind today, what has happened to love for God and for the Bible? (b) How can we prevent our love from cooling off?

*What Does the Bible Really Teach?*

¹⁴ Another way to keep your love for Jehovah burning brightly is to pray regularly. (1 Thessalonians 5:17) In Chapter 17 of this book, we learned that prayer is a precious gift from God. Just as human relationships thrive on regular, open communication, so our relationship with Jehovah stays warm and alive when we pray to him regularly. It is vital that we never let our prayers become mechanical—mere routine words that we repeat over and over without real feeling or meaning. We need to speak to Jehovah as a child would talk to a beloved father. We want to speak with respect, of course, but openly, honestly, and from the heart. (Psalm 62:8) Yes, personal Bible study and heartfelt prayer are vital aspects of our worship, and they help us to remain in God's love.

## FIND JOY IN YOUR WORSHIP

¹⁵ Personal Bible study and prayer are acts of worship that we may carry out in private. Now, however, let us consider an aspect of worship that we carry out publicly: speaking to others about our beliefs. Have you already shared some Bible truths with others? If

**14. How can prayer help us to keep our love for Jehovah alive?**
**15, 16. Why may we rightly view the Kingdom-preaching work as a privilege and a treasure?**

so, you have enjoyed a wonderful privilege. (Luke 1:74) When we share the truths we have learned about Jehovah God, we are taking up a very important assignment given to all true Christians—that of preaching the good news of God's Kingdom.—Matthew 24:14; 28:19, 20.

¹⁶ The apostle Paul viewed his ministry as something precious, calling it a treasure. (2 Corinthians 4:7) Talking to people about Jehovah God and his purposes is the best work you could do. It is service to the best Master, and it brings the best benefits possible. By engaging in this activity, you are helping honesthearted people to draw close to our heavenly Father and to get on the road to everlasting life! What work could be more satisfying? Furthermore, witnessing about Jehovah and his Word increases your own faith and strengthens your love for him. And Jehovah appreciates your efforts. (Hebrews 6:10) Staying busy in such work helps you to remain in God's love.—1 Corinthians 15:58.

¹⁷ It is important to remember that the Kingdom-preaching work is urgent. The Bible says: "Preach the word, be at it urgently." (2 Timothy 4:2) Why is doing

**17. Why is the Christian ministry urgent today?**

*What Does the Bible Really Teach?*

this so urgent today? God's Word tells us: "The great day of Jehovah is near. It is near, and there is a hurrying of it very much." (Zephaniah 1:14) Yes, the time is coming quickly when Jehovah will bring this whole system of things to its end. People need to be warned! They need to know that now is the time to choose Jehovah as their Sovereign. The end "will not be late." —Habakkuk 2:3.

¹⁸ Jehovah wants us to worship him publicly in association with true Christians. That is why his Word says: "Let us consider one another to incite to love and fine works, not forsaking the gathering of ourselves together, as some have the custom, but encouraging one another, and all the more so as you behold the day drawing near." (Hebrews 10:24, 25) When we gather with fellow believers at Christian meetings, we have a wonderful opportunity to praise and worship our beloved God. We also build one another up and encourage one another.

¹⁹ As we associate with other worshipers of Jehovah, we strengthen the bonds of love and friendship in the

18. Why should we worship Jehovah publicly in association with true Christians?
19. How can we work to strengthen the bonds of love in the Christian congregation?

congregation. It is important that we look for the good in one another, as Jehovah looks for the good in us. Do not expect perfection from your fellow believers. Remember that all are at different stages of spiritual growth and that every one of us makes mistakes. (Colossians 3:13) Seek to build close friendships with those who love Jehovah intensely, and you will find yourself growing spiritually. Yes, worshiping Jehovah with your spiritual brothers and sisters will help you to remain in God's love. How does Jehovah reward those who worship him faithfully and thus remain in his love?

## REACH OUT FOR "THE REAL LIFE"

20 Jehovah rewards his faithful servants with life, but life of what kind? Well, are you really living now? Most of us would say that the answer is obvious. After all, we breathe, we eat, and we drink. Surely we must be living. And in our happier moments, we may even say, "Now this is *really* living!" However, the Bible indicates that in an important sense, no human today is *really* living.

21 God's Word urges us to "get a firm hold on the real life." (1 Timothy 6:19) Those words indicate that "the

**20, 21. What is "the real life," and why is it a wonderful hope?**

*What Does the Bible Really Teach?*

real life" is something we hope to attain in the future. Yes, when we are perfect, we will be alive in the fullest sense of the word, for we will be living as God originally intended us to live. When we are living on a paradise earth in complete health, peace, and happiness, we will at last enjoy "the real life"—everlasting life. (1 Timothy 6:12) Is that not a wonderful hope?

22 How can we "get a firm hold on the real life"? In the same context, Paul urged Christians "to work at good" and "to be rich in fine works." (1 Timothy 6:18) Clearly, then, much depends on how we apply the truths we have learned from the Bible. But did Paul mean that we *earn* "the real life" by performing good works? No, for such marvelous prospects really depend on our receiving "undeserved kindness" from God. (Romans 5:15) However, Jehovah delights in rewarding those who serve him faithfully. He wants to see you live "the real life." Such a happy, peaceful, everlasting life lies ahead for those who remain in God's love.

23 Each of us does well to ask himself, 'Am I worshiping God in the way he has set out in the Bible?' If we

22. How can you "get a firm hold on the real life"?
23. Why is it essential to remain in God's love?

make sure, day by day, that the answer is yes, then we are on the right path. We can be confident that Jehovah is our refuge. He will keep his faithful people safe through the last troubled days of this old system of things. Jehovah will also deliver us into the glorious new system of things now near. How thrilled we will be to see that time! And how delighted we will be that we made the right choices during these last days! If you make such choices now, you will enjoy "the real life," life as Jehovah God meant it to be, throughout all eternity!

---

## WHAT THE BIBLE TEACHES

- We show genuine love for God by observing his commandments and applying his principles.—1 John 5:3.

- Studying God's Word, praying to Jehovah in a heartfelt way, teaching others about him, and worshiping him at Christian meetings will help us to remain in God's love.—Matthew 24:14; 28:19, 20; John 17:3; 1 Thessalonians 5:17; Hebrews 10:24, 25.

- Those who remain in God's love have the hope of enjoying "the real life."—1 Timothy 6:12, 19; Jude 21.

---

*What Does the Bible Really Teach?*

# APPENDIX

# The Divine Name
# —Its Use and Its Meaning

IN YOUR copy of the Bible, how is Psalm 83:18 translated? The *New World Translation of the Holy Scriptures* renders this verse: "That people may know that you, whose name is Jehovah, you alone are the Most High over all the earth." A number of other Bible translations give similar renderings. However, many translations leave out the name Jehovah, replacing it with such titles as "Lord" or "Eternal." What belongs in this verse? A title or the name Jehovah?

This verse speaks about a name. In the original Hebrew in which much of the Bible was written, a unique personal name appears here. It is spelled יהוה (YHWH) in Hebrew letters. In English, the common rendering of that name is "Jehovah." Does that name occur in only one Bible verse? No. It appears in the original text of the Hebrew Scriptures nearly 7,000 times!

How important is God's name? Consider the model prayer that Jesus Christ gave. It begins this way: "Our Father in the heavens, let your name be sanctified." (Matthew 6:9) Later, Jesus prayed to God: "Father, glorify your name." In response, God spoke from heaven, saying: "I both glorified it and will glorify it again." (John 12:28)

*What Does the Bible Really Teach?*

Clearly, God's name is of the utmost importance. Why, then, have some translators left this name out of their translations of the Bible and replaced it with titles?

There seem to be two main reasons. First, many claim that the name should not be used because the original way to pronounce it is unknown today. Ancient Hebrew was written without vowels. Therefore, no one today can say for sure exactly how people of Bible times pronounced YHWH. However, should this prevent us from using God's name? In Bible times, the name Jesus may have been pronounced Yeshua or possibly Yehoshua—no one can say for certain. Yet, people the world over today use different forms of the name Jesus, pronouncing it in the way that is common in their language. They do not hesitate to use the name just because they do not know its first-century pronunciation. Similarly, if you were to travel to a foreign land, you might well find that your own name sounds quite different in another tongue. Hence, uncertainty about the ancient pronunciation of God's name is no reason for not using it.

A second reason often given for omitting God's name from the Bible involves a long-standing tradition of the Jews. Many of them hold that God's name should never be pronounced. This belief is evidently based on a misapplication of a Bible law that states: "You must not take up the name of Jehovah your God in a worthless way, for Jehovah will not leave the one unpunished who takes up his name in a worthless way."—Exodus 20:7.

This law forbids the misuse of God's name. But does it forbid the respectful use of his name? Not at all. The writers of the Hebrew Bible (the "Old Testament") were all faithful men who lived by the Law that God gave to the ancient Israelites. Yet, they made frequent use of God's name. For instance, they included it in many psalms that were sung out loud by crowds of worshipers. Jehovah God even instructed his worshipers to call upon his name, and faithful ones obeyed. (Joel 2:32; Acts 2:21) Hence, Christians today do not hesitate to use God's name respectfully, as Jesus surely did.—John 17:26.

In replacing God's name with titles, Bible translators make a serious mistake. They make God seem remote and impersonal, whereas the Bible urges humans to cultivate "intimacy with Jehovah." (Psalm 25:14) Think of an intimate friend of yours. How close would you really be if you never learned your friend's name? Similarly, when people are kept in ignorance about God's name, Jehovah, how can they become truly close to God? Furthermore, when people do not use God's name, they also lack knowledge of its wonderful meaning. What does the divine name mean?

God himself explained the meaning of his name to his faithful servant Moses. When Moses asked about God's name, Jehovah replied: "I shall prove to be what I shall prove to be." (Exodus 3:14) Rotherham's translation renders those words: "I Will Become whatsoever I please." So Jehovah can become whatever is needed in order to fulfill his purposes.

Suppose that you could become whatever you wanted to become? What would you do for your friends? If one of them became seriously ill, you could become a skilled doctor and perform a cure. If another suffered a financial loss, you could become a wealthy benefactor and come to his rescue. The truth is, though, that you are limited in what you can become. All of us are. As you study the Bible, you will be amazed to see how Jehovah becomes *whatever* is needed in order to fulfill his promises. And it pleases him to use his power in behalf of those who love him. (2 Chronicles 16:9) These beautiful facets of Jehovah's personality are lost to those who do not know his name.

Clearly, the name Jehovah belongs in the Bible. Knowing its meaning and using it freely in our worship are powerful aids in drawing closer to our heavenly Father, Jehovah.*

---

* For more information on God's name, its meaning, and reasons why it should be used in worship, see the brochure *The Divine Name That Will Endure Forever,* published by Jehovah's Witnesses.

# How Daniel's Prophecy Foretells the Messiah's Arrival

THE prophet Daniel lived more than 500 years before the birth of Jesus. Nevertheless, Jehovah revealed to Daniel information that would make it possible to pinpoint the time when Jesus would be anointed, or appointed, as the Messiah, or Christ. Daniel was told: "You should know and have the insight that from the going forth of the word to restore and to rebuild Jerusalem until Messiah the Leader, there will be seven weeks, also sixty-two weeks." —Daniel 9:25.

To determine the time of the Messiah's arrival, first we need to learn the starting point of the period leading to the Messiah. According to the prophecy, it is "from the going forth of the word to restore and to rebuild Jerusalem." When did this "going forth of the word" take place? According to the Bible writer Nehemiah, the word went forth to rebuild the walls around Jerusalem "in the twentieth year of Artaxerxes the king." (Nehemiah 2:1, 5-8) Historians confirm that the year 474 B.C.E. was Artaxerxes' first full year as ruler. Therefore, the 20th year of his rule was 455 B.C.E. Now we have the starting point for Daniel's Messianic prophecy, that is, 455 B.C.E.

Daniel indicates how long the time period leading to the arrival of "Messiah the Leader" would last. The prophecy mentions "seven weeks, also sixty-two weeks"—a total of 69 weeks. How long is this period of time? Several Bible translations note that these are, not weeks of seven days, but weeks of years. That is, each week represents seven years. This concept of weeks of years, or seven-year units,

## "SEVENTY WEEKS"

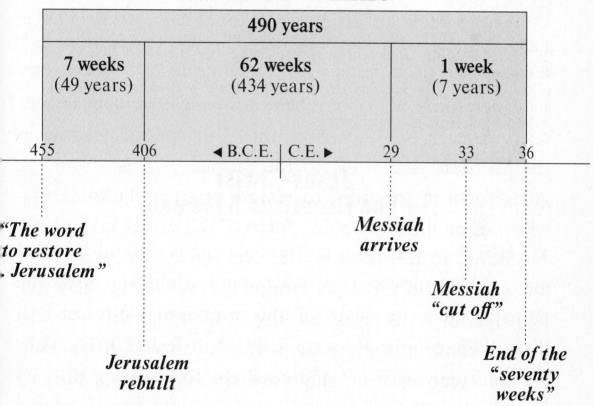

| 490 years | | |
|---|---|---|
| 7 weeks (49 years) | 62 weeks (434 years) | 1 week (7 years) |

455     406     ◄ B.C.E. | C.E. ►     29     33     36

*"The word to restore Jerusalem"*

*Messiah arrives*

*Messiah "cut off"*

*Jerusalem rebuilt*

*End of the "seventy weeks"*

was familiar to Jews of ancient times. For instance, they observed a Sabbath year every seventh year. (Exodus 23:10, 11) Therefore, the prophetic 69 weeks amount to 69 units of 7 years each, or a total of 483 years.

Now all we must do is count. If we count from 455 B.C.E., 483 years takes us to the year 29 C.E. That was exactly the year when Jesus was baptized and became the Messiah!* (Luke 3:1, 2, 21, 22) Is that not a remarkable fulfillment of Bible prophecy?

---

* From 455 B.C.E. to 1 B.C.E. is 454 years. From 1 B.C.E. to 1 C.E. is one year (there was no zero year). And from 1 C.E. to 29 C.E. is 28 years. Adding these three figures gives us the total of 483 years. Jesus was "cut off" in death in 33 C.E., during the 70th week of years. (Daniel 9:24, 26) See *Pay Attention to Daniel's Prophecy!* chapter 11, and *Insight on the Scriptures,* Volume 2, pages 899-901. Both are published by Jehovah's Witnesses.

## Jesus Christ —The Promised Messiah

TO HELP us identify the Messiah, Jehovah God inspired many Bible prophets to provide details about the birth, the ministry, and the death of this promised Deliverer. All these Bible prophecies were fulfilled in Jesus Christ. They are amazingly accurate and detailed. To illustrate this, let us consider a few prophecies that foretold events related to the Messiah's birth and childhood.

# PROPHECIES REGARDING THE MESSIAH

| EVENT | PROPHECY | FULFILLMENT |
|---|---|---|
| Born of the tribe of Judah | Genesis 49:10 | Luke 3:23-33 |
| Born of a virgin | Isaiah 7:14 | Matthew 1:18-25 |
| Descended from King David | Isaiah 9:7 | Matthew 1:1, 6-17 |
| Declared by Jehovah to be his Son | Psalm 2:7 | Matthew 3:17 |
| Not believed in | Isaiah 53:1 | John 12:37, 38 |
| Entered Jerusalem riding an ass | Zechariah 9:9 | Matthew 21:1-9 |
| Betrayed by a close associate | Psalm 41:9 | John 13:18, 21-30 |
| Betrayed for 30 silver pieces | Zechariah 11:12 | Matthew 26:14-16 |
| Silent before his accusers | Isaiah 53:7 | Matthew 27:11-14 |
| Lots cast for his garments | Psalm 22:18 | Matthew 27:35 |
| Reviled while on the stake | Psalm 22:7, 8 | Matthew 27:39-43 |
| None of his bones broken | Psalm 34:20 | John 19:33, 36 |
| Buried with the rich | Isaiah 53:9 | Matthew 27:57-60 |
| Raised before corruption | Psalm 16:10 | Acts 2:24, 27 |
| Exalted to God's right hand | Psalm 110:1 | Acts 7:56 |

The prophet Isaiah foretold that the Messiah would be a descendant of King David. (Isaiah 9:7) Jesus was indeed born in David's line.—Matthew 1:1, 6-17.

Micah, another prophet of God, foretold that this child would eventually become a ruler and that he would be born in "Bethlehem Ephrathah." (Micah 5:2) At the time of Jesus' birth, there were two towns in Israel that were named Bethlehem. One was situated near Nazareth in the northern region of the country, and the other, near Jerusalem in Judah. Bethlehem near Jerusalem was formerly called Ephrathah. Jesus was born in that town, exactly as the prophecy foretold!—Matthew 2:1.

Another Bible prophecy foretold that the Son of God would be called "out of Egypt." The child Jesus was taken into Egypt. He was brought back after the death of Herod, thus fulfilling the prophecy.—Hosea 11:1; Matthew 2:15.

In the chart on page 255, the scriptures listed under the heading "Prophecy" contain details concerning the Messiah. Please compare these with the scriptures listed under the heading "Fulfillment." Doing so will further strengthen your faith in the truthfulness of God's Word.

While you examine these scriptures, keep in mind that those of a prophetic nature were written down hundreds of years before Jesus' birth. Jesus stated: "All the things written in the law of Moses and in the Prophets and Psalms about me must be fulfilled." (Luke 24:44) As you can verify in your own copy of the Bible, fulfilled they were—in every detail!

*What Does the Bible Really Teach?*

# The Truth About the Father, the Son, and the Holy Spirit

PEOPLE who believe the Trinity teaching say that God consists of three persons—the Father, the Son, and the Holy Spirit. Each of these three persons is said to be equal to the others, almighty, and without beginning. According to the Trinity doctrine, therefore, the Father is God, the Son is God, and the Holy Spirit is God, yet there is only one God.

Many who believe the Trinity admit that they are not able to explain this teaching. Still, they may feel that it is taught in the Bible. It is worth noting that the word "Trinity" never occurs in the Bible. But is the idea of a Trinity found there? To answer this question, let us look at a scripture that supporters often cite to uphold the Trinity.

## "THE WORD WAS GOD"

John 1:1 states: "In the beginning was the Word, and the Word was with God, and the Word was God." (*King James Version*) Later in the same chapter, the apostle John clearly shows that "the Word" is Jesus. (John 1:14) Since the Word is called God, however, some conclude that the Son and the Father must be part of the same God.

Bear in mind that this part of the Bible was originally written in Greek. Later, translators rendered the Greek text into other languages. A number of Bible translators, though, did not use the phrase "the Word was God." Why not? Based on their knowledge of Biblical Greek, those translators concluded that the phrase "the Word was God" should be translated differently. How? Here are a few examples: "The Logos [Word] was divine." (*A New Translation of the Bible*) "The Word was a god." (*The New Testament in an Improved Version*) "The Word was with God and shared his nature." (*The Translator's New Testament*) According to these translations, the Word is not God himself.* Instead, because of his high position among Jehovah's creatures, the Word is referred to as "a god." Here the term "god" means "mighty one."

## GET MORE FACTS

Most people do not know Biblical Greek. So how can you know what the apostle John really meant? Think of this example: A schoolteacher explains a subject to his students. Afterward, the students differ on how to understand the explanation. How can the students resolve the matter? They could ask the teacher for more information. No doubt, learning additional facts would help them to understand the subject better. Similarly, to grasp the meaning of John 1:1, you can look in the Gospel of John for more informa-

* For a consideration of the rules of Greek grammar that apply to John 1:1, see pages 26-9 of the brochure *Should You Believe in the Trinity?* published by Jehovah's Witnesses.

*What Does the Bible Really Teach?*

tion on Jesus' position. Learning additional facts on this subject will help you to draw the right conclusion.

For instance, consider what John further writes in chapter 1, verse 18: "No man has seen [Almighty] God at any time." However, humans have seen Jesus, the Son, for John says: "The Word [Jesus] was made flesh, and dwelt among us, and we beheld his glory." (John 1:14, *KJ*) How, then, could the Son be part of Almighty God? John also states that the Word was *"with* God." But how can an individual be *with* someone and at the same time *be* that person? Moreover, as recorded at John 17:3, Jesus makes a clear distinction between himself and his heavenly Father. He calls his Father "the only true God." And toward the end of his Gospel, John sums up matters by saying: "These have been written down that you may believe that Jesus is the Christ the Son of God." (John 20:31) Notice that Jesus is called, not God, but the Son of God. This additional information provided in the Gospel of John shows how John 1:1 should be understood. Jesus, the Word, is "a god" in the sense that he has a high position but is not the same as Almighty God.

## CONFIRM THE FACTS

Think again about the example of the schoolteacher and the students. Imagine that some still have doubts, even after listening to the teacher's additional explanation. What could they do? They could turn to another teacher for further information on the same subject. If the second teacher confirms the explanation of the first one, the doubts of most students may be put to rest. Similarly, if you are not sure what the Bible writer John was really saying about the relationship between Jesus and Almighty God, you could turn to another Bible writer for further information. Consider what was written by Matthew, for example. Regarding the end of this system of things, he quotes Jesus as saying: "Concerning that day and hour nobody knows, neither the angels of the heavens nor the Son, but only the Father." (Matthew 24:36) How do these words confirm that Jesus is not Almighty God?

Jesus says that the Father knows more than the Son does. If Jesus were part of Almighty God, however, he would know the same facts as his Father. So, then, the Son and the Father cannot be equal. Yet, some will say: 'Jesus had two natures. Here he speaks as a man.' But even if that were so, what about the holy spirit? If it is part of the same God as the Father, why does Jesus not say that it knows what the Father knows?

As you continue your Bible studies, you will become familiar with many more Bible passages that have a bearing on this subject. They confirm the truth about the Father, the Son, and the holy spirit.—Psalm 90:2; Acts 7:55; Colossians 1:15.

*What Does the Bible Really Teach?*

# Why True Christians Do Not Use the Cross in Worship

THE cross is loved and respected by millions of people. *The Encyclopædia Britannica* calls the cross "the principal symbol of the Christian religion." Nevertheless, true Christians do not use the cross in worship. Why not?

An important reason is that Jesus Christ did not die on a cross. The Greek word generally translated "cross" is *stau·ros'*. It basically means "an upright pale or stake." *The Companion Bible* points out: "[*Stau·ros'*] never means *two* pieces of timber placed across one another at any angle . . . There is nothing in the Greek of the [New Testament] even to imply two pieces of timber."

In several texts, Bible writers use another word for the instrument of Jesus' death. It is the Greek word *xy'lon*. (Acts 5:30; 10:39; 13:29; Galatians 3:13; 1 Peter 2:24) This word simply means "timber" or "a stick, club, or tree."

Explaining why a simple stake was often used for executions, the book *Das Kreuz und die Kreuzigung* (The Cross and the Crucifixion), by Hermann Fulda, states: "Trees were not everywhere available at the places chosen for public execution. So a simple beam was sunk into the ground. On this the outlaws, with hands raised upward and often also with their feet, were bound or nailed."

The most convincing proof of all, however, comes from God's Word. The apostle Paul says: "Christ by purchase released us from the curse of the Law by becoming a curse instead of us, because it is written: 'Accursed is every man hanged upon a stake ["a tree," *King James Version*].'" (Galatians 3:13) Here Paul quotes Deuteronomy 21:22, 23, which clearly refers to a stake, not a cross. Since such a means of execution made the person "a curse," it would not be proper for Christians to decorate their homes with images of Christ impaled.

There is no evidence that for the first 300 years after Christ's death, those claiming to be Christians used the cross in worship. In the fourth century, however, pagan Emperor Constantine became a convert to apostate Christianity and promoted the cross as its symbol. Whatever Constantine's motives, the cross had nothing to do with Jesus Christ. The cross is, in fact, pagan in origin. The *New Catholic Encyclopedia* admits: "The cross is found in both pre-Christian and non-Christian cultures." Various other authorities have linked the cross with nature worship and pagan sex rites.

Why, then, was this pagan symbol promoted? Apparently, to make it easier for pagans to accept "Christianity." Nevertheless, devotion to any pagan symbol is clearly condemned by the Bible. (2 Corinthians 6:14-18) The Scrip-

*What Does the Bible Really Teach?*

tures also forbid all forms of idolatry. (Exodus 20:4, 5; 1 Corinthians 10:14) With very good reason, therefore, true Christians do not use the cross in worship.*

---

* For a more detailed discussion of the cross, see pages 89-93 of the book *Reasoning From the Scriptures,* published by Jehovah's Witnesses.

## The Lord's Evening Meal —An Observance That Honors God

CHRISTIANS are commanded to observe the Memorial of Christ's death. This observance is also called "the Lord's evening meal." (1 Corinthians 11:20) What is so significant about it? When and how should it be observed?

Jesus Christ instituted this observance on the night of the Jewish Passover in 33 C.E. The Passover was a celebration held just once a year, on the 14th day of the Jewish month Nisan. To calculate that date, the Jews evidently waited for the spring equinox. This is the day when there are approximately 12 hours of daylight and 12 hours of darkness. The first observable new moon nearest to the spring equinox marked the beginning of Nisan. Passover came 14 days later, after sunset.

Jesus celebrated the Passover with his apostles, dismissed Judas Iscariot, and then instituted the Lord's

Evening Meal. This meal replaced the Jewish Passover and therefore should be observed only once a year.

The Gospel of Matthew reports: "Jesus took a loaf and, after saying a blessing, he broke it and, giving it to the disciples, he said: 'Take, eat. This means my body.' Also, he took a cup and, having given thanks, he gave it to them, saying: 'Drink out of it, all of you; for this means my "blood of the covenant," which is to be poured out in behalf of many for forgiveness of sins.'"—Matthew 26:26-28.

Some believe that Jesus turned the bread into his literal flesh and the wine into his blood. However, Jesus' fleshly body was still intact when he offered this bread. Were Jesus' apostles really eating his literal flesh and drinking his blood? No, for that would have been cannibalism and a violation of God's law. (Genesis 9:3, 4; Leviticus 17:10) According to Luke 22:20, Jesus said: "This cup means the new covenant by virtue of my blood, which is to be poured out in your behalf." Did that cup literally become "the new covenant"? That would be impossible, since a covenant is an agreement, not a tangible object.

Hence, both the bread and the wine are only symbols. The bread symbolizes Christ's perfect body. Jesus used a loaf of bread left over from the Passover meal. The loaf was made without any leaven, or yeast. (Exodus 12:8) The Bible uses leaven as a symbol of sin or corruption. The

*What Does the Bible Really Teach?*

bread therefore represents the perfect body that Jesus sacrificed. It was free of sin.—Matthew 16:11, 12; 1 Corinthians 5:6, 7; 1 Peter 2:22; 1 John 2:1, 2.

The red wine represents Jesus' blood. That blood makes valid the new covenant. Jesus said that his blood was poured out "for forgiveness of sins." Humans can thus become clean in God's eyes and can enter into the new covenant with Jehovah. (Hebrews 9:14; 10:16, 17) This covenant, or contract, makes it possible for 144,000 faithful Christians to go to heaven. There they will serve as kings and priests for the blessing of all mankind.—Genesis 22:18; Jeremiah 31:31-33; 1 Peter 2:9; Revelation 5:9, 10; 14:1-3.

Who should partake of these Memorial emblems? Logically, only those in the new covenant—that is, those who have the hope of going to heaven—should partake of the bread and the wine. God's holy spirit convinces such ones that they have been selected to be heavenly kings. (Romans 8:16) They are also in the Kingdom covenant with Jesus.—Luke 22:29.

What about those who have the hope of living forever in Paradise on earth? They obey Jesus' command and attend the Lord's Evening Meal, but they come as respectful observers, not partakers. Once a year after sundown on Nisan 14, Jehovah's Witnesses observe the Lord's Evening Meal. Although only a few thousand worldwide profess to have the heavenly hope, this observance is precious to all Christians. It is an occasion when all can reflect upon the superlative love of Jehovah God and Jesus Christ.—John 3:16.

# "Soul" and "Spirit" —What Do These Terms Really Mean?

WHEN you hear the terms "soul" and "spirit," what comes to your mind? Many believe that these words mean something invisible and immortal that exists inside us. They think that at death this invisible part of a human leaves the body and lives on. Since this belief is so widespread, many are surprised to learn that it is not at all what the Bible teaches. What, then, is the soul, and what is the spirit, according to God's Word?

## "SOUL" AS USED IN THE BIBLE

First, consider the soul. You may remember that the Bible was originally written mainly in Hebrew and Greek. When writing about the soul, the Bible writers used the Hebrew word *ne'phesh* or the Greek word *psy·khe'*. These two words occur well over 800 times in the Scriptures, and the *New World Translation* consistently renders them "soul." When you examine the way "soul" or "souls" is used in the Bible, it becomes evident that this word basically refers to

*What Does the Bible Really Teach?*

(1) people, (2) animals, or (3) the life that a person or an animal enjoys. Let us consider some scriptures that present these three different senses.

*People.* "In Noah's days . . . a few people, that is, eight souls, were carried safely through the water." (1 Peter 3:20) Here the word "souls" clearly stands for people —Noah, his wife, his three sons, and their wives. Exodus 16:16 mentions instructions given to the Israelites regarding the gathering of manna. They were told: "Pick up some of it . . . according to the number of the souls that each of you has in his tent." So the amount of manna that was gathered was based upon the number of people in each family. Some other Biblical examples of the application of "soul" or "souls" to a person or to people are found at Genesis 46:18; Joshua 11:11; Acts 27:37; and Romans 13:1.

*Animals.* In the Bible's creation account, we read: "God went on to say: 'Let the waters swarm forth a swarm of living souls and let flying creatures fly over the earth upon the face of the expanse of the heavens.' And God went on to say: 'Let the earth put forth living souls according to their kinds, domestic animal and moving animal and wild beast of the earth according to its kind.' And it came to be so." (Genesis 1:20, 24) In this passage, fish, domestic animals, and wild beasts are all referred to by the same word—"souls." Birds and other animals are called souls at Genesis 9:10; Leviticus 11:46; and Numbers 31:28.

*Life as a person.* Sometimes the word "soul" means one's life as a person. Jehovah told Moses: "All the men who were hunting for your soul are dead." (Exodus 4:19) What were Moses' enemies hunting for? They were seeking to take Moses' life. Earlier, while Rachel was giving birth to her son Benjamin, "her soul was going out (because she died)." (Genesis 35:16-19) At that moment, Rachel lost her life. Consider also Jesus' words: "I am the fine shepherd; the fine shepherd surrenders his soul in behalf of the sheep." (John 10:11) Jesus gave his soul, or life, in behalf of mankind. In these Bible passages, the word "soul" clearly refers to life as a person. You will find more examples of this sense of "soul" at 1 Kings 17:17-23; Matthew 10:39; John 15:13; and Acts 20:10.

A further study of God's Word will show you that nowhere in the entire Bible are the terms "immortal" or "everlasting" linked with the word "soul." Instead, the Scriptures state that a soul is mortal, meaning that it dies. (Ezekiel 18:4, 20) Therefore, the Bible calls someone who has died simply a "dead soul."—Leviticus 21:11.

## THE "SPIRIT" IDENTIFIED

Let us now consider the Bible's use of the term "spirit." Some people think that "spirit" is just another word for

*What Does the Bible Really Teach?*

"soul." However, that is not the case. The Bible makes clear that "spirit" and "soul" refer to two different things. How do they differ?

Bible writers used the Hebrew word *ru'ach* or the Greek word *pneu'ma* when writing about the "spirit." The Scriptures themselves indicate the meaning of those words. For instance, Psalm 104:29 states: "If you [Jehovah] take away their spirit [*ru'ach*], they expire, and back to their dust they go." And James 2:26 notes that "the body without spirit [*pneu'ma*] is dead." In these verses, then, "spirit" refers to that which gives life to a body. Without spirit, the body is dead. Therefore, in the Bible the word *ru'ach* is translated not only as "spirit" but also as "force," or life-force. For example, concerning the Flood in Noah's day, God said: "I am bringing the deluge of waters upon the earth to bring to ruin all flesh in which the force [*ru'ach*] of life is active from under the heavens." (Genesis 6:17; 7:15, 22) "Spirit" thus refers to an invisible force (the spark of life) that animates all living creatures.

The soul and the spirit are not the same. The body needs the spirit in much the same way as a radio needs electricity—in order to function. To illustrate this further, think of a portable radio. When you put batteries in a portable radio and turn it on, the electricity stored in the batteries brings the radio to life, so to speak. Without batteries, however, the radio is dead. So is another kind of radio when it is unplugged from an electric outlet. Similarly, the spirit is the force that brings our body to life. Also, like electricity, the spirit has no feeling and cannot think. It is an impersonal force. But without that spirit, or life-force, our bodies "expire, and back to their dust they go," as the psalmist stated.

Speaking about man's death, Ecclesiastes 12:7 states: "The dust [of his body] returns to the earth just as it happened to be and the spirit itself returns to the true God who gave it." When the spirit, or life-force, leaves the body, the body dies and returns to where it came from —the earth. Comparably, the life-force returns to where it came from—God. (Job 34:14, 15; Psalm 36:9) This does not mean that the life-force actually travels to heaven. Rather, it means that for someone who dies, any hope of future life rests with Jehovah God. His life is in God's hands, so to speak. Only by God's power can the spirit, or life-force, be given back so that a person may live again.

How comforting it is to know that this is exactly what God will do for all of those resting in "the memorial tombs"! (John 5:28, 29) At the time of the resurrection, Jehovah will form a new body for a person sleeping in death and bring it to life by putting spirit, or life-force, in it. What a joyful day that will be!

*What Does the Bible Really Teach?*

If you would like to learn more about the terms "soul" and "spirit" as used in the Bible, you will find valuable information in the brochure *What Happens to Us When We Die?* and on pages 375-84 of the book *Reasoning From the Scriptures,* both published by Jehovah's Witnesses.

## What Are Sheol and Hades?

IN ITS original languages, the Bible uses the Hebrew word *she'ohl'* and its Greek equivalent *hai'des* more than 70 times. Both words are related to death. Some Bible translations render them as "grave," "hell," or "pit." However, in most languages there are no words that convey the precise sense of these Hebrew and Greek words. The *New World Translation* therefore uses the words "Sheol" and "Hades." What do these words really mean? Let us note how they are used in different Bible passages.

Ecclesiastes 9:10 states: "There is no work nor devising nor knowledge nor wisdom in Sheol, the place to which you are going." Does this mean that Sheol refers to a specific, or individual, grave site where we may have buried a loved one? No. When the Bible refers to a specific burial place, or grave, it uses other Hebrew and Greek words, not *she'ohl'* and *hai'des.* (Genesis 23:7-9; Matthew 28:1) Also, the Bible does not use the word "Sheol" for a grave where several individuals are buried together, such as a family grave or a mass grave.—Genesis 49:30, 31.

To what kind of place, then, does "Sheol" refer? God's Word indicates that "Sheol," or "Hades," refers to something much more than even a large mass grave. For instance, Isaiah 5:14 notes that Sheol is "spacious and has opened its mouth wide beyond bounds." Although Sheol has already swallowed, so to speak, countless dead people, it always seems to hunger for more. (Proverbs 30:15, 16) Unlike any literal burial site, which can hold only a limited number of the dead, "Sheol and the place of destruction themselves do not get satisfied." (Proverbs 27:20) Sheol never becomes full. It has no limits. Sheol, or Hades, is thus not a literal place in a specific location. Rather, it is the common grave of dead mankind, the figurative location where most of mankind sleep in death.

The Bible teaching of the resurrection helps us to gain further insight into the meaning of "Sheol" and "Hades." God's Word associates Sheol and Hades with the sort of death from which there will be a resurrection.* (Job 14:13; Acts 2:31; Revelation 20:13) God's Word also shows that those in Sheol, or Hades, include not only those who have

---

* In contrast, the dead who will not be raised are described as being, not in Sheol, or Hades, but "in Gehenna." (Matthew 5:30; 10:28; 23:33) Like Sheol and Hades, Gehenna is not a literal place.

*What Does the Bible Really Teach?*

served Jehovah but also many who have not served him. (Genesis 37:35; Psalm 55:15) Therefore, the Bible teaches that there will be "a resurrection of both the righteous and the unrighteous."—Acts 24:15.

# Judgment Day—What Is It?

HOW do you picture Judgment Day? Many think that one by one, billions of souls will be brought before the throne of God. There, judgment will be passed upon each individual. Some will be rewarded with heavenly bliss, and others will be condemned to eternal torment. However, the Bible paints quite a different picture of this period of time. God's Word portrays it, not as a terrifying time, but as a time of hope and restoration.

At Revelation 20:11, 12, we read the apostle John's description of Judgment Day: "I saw a great white throne and the one seated on it. From before him the earth and the heaven fled away, and no place was found for them. And I saw the dead, the great and the small, standing before the throne, and scrolls were opened. But another scroll was opened; it is the scroll of life. And the dead were judged out of those things written in the scrolls according to their deeds." Who is the Judge described here?

Jehovah God is the ultimate Judge of mankind.

However, he delegates the actual work of judging. According to Acts 17:31, the apostle Paul said that God "has set a day in which he purposes to judge the inhabited earth in righteousness by a man whom he has appointed." This appointed Judge is the resurrected Jesus Christ. (John 5: 22) When, though, does Judgment Day begin? How long does it last?

The book of Revelation shows that Judgment Day begins after the war of Armageddon, when Satan's system on earth will be destroyed.* (Revelation 16:14, 16; 19:19–20:3) After Armageddon, Satan and his demons will be imprisoned in an abyss for a thousand years. During that time, the 144,000 heavenly joint heirs will be judges and will rule "as kings with the Christ for a thousand years." (Revelation 14:1-3; 20:1-4; Romans 8:17) Judgment Day is not some hurried event lasting a mere 24 hours. It lasts a thousand years.

During that thousand-year period, Jesus Christ will "judge the living and the dead." (2 Timothy 4:1) "The living" will be the "great crowd" that survives Armageddon. (Revelation 7:9-17) The apostle John also saw "the dead . . . standing before the throne" of judgment. As Jesus promised, "those in the memorial tombs will hear

---

* Regarding Armageddon, please see *Insight on the Scriptures,* Volume 1, pages 594-5, 1037-8, and chapter 20 of *Worship the Only True God,* both published by Jehovah's Witnesses.

[Christ's] voice and come out" by means of a resurrection. (John 5:28, 29; Acts 24:15) But on what basis will all be judged?

According to the apostle John's vision, "scrolls were opened," and "the dead were judged out of those things written in the scrolls according to their deeds." Are these scrolls the record of people's past deeds? No, the judgment will not focus on what people did before they died. How do we know that? The Bible says: "He who has died has been acquitted from his sin." (Romans 6:7) Those resurrected thus come to life with a clean slate, so to speak. The scrolls must therefore represent God's further requirements. To live forever, both Armageddon survivors and resurrected ones will have to obey God's commandments, including whatever new requirements Jehovah might reveal during the thousand years. Thus, individuals will be judged on the basis of what they do *during* Judgment Day.

Judgment Day will give billions of people their first opportunity to learn about God's will and to conform to it. This means that a large-scale educational work will take place. Indeed, "righteousness is what the inhabitants of the productive land will certainly learn." (Isaiah 26:9) However, not all will be willing to conform to God's will. Isaiah 26:10 says: "Though the wicked one should be shown favor, he simply will not learn righteousness. In the land of straightforwardness he will act unjustly and will not see the eminence of Jehovah." These wicked ones will be put to death permanently during Judgment Day.—Isaiah 65:20.

By the end of Judgment Day, surviving humans will have "come to life" fully as perfect humans. (Revelation 20:5) Judgment Day will thus see the restoration of mankind to its original perfect state. (1 Corinthians 15:24-28) Then a final test will take place. Satan will be released from his imprisonment and allowed to try to mislead mankind one last time. (Revelation 20:3, 7-10) Those who resist him will enjoy the complete fulfillment of the Bible's promise: "The righteous themselves will possess the earth, and they will reside forever upon it." (Psalm 37:29) Yes, Judgment Day will be a blessing to all faithful mankind!

# 1914—A Significant Year in Bible Prophecy

DECADES in advance, Bible students proclaimed that there would be significant developments in 1914. What were these, and what evidence points to 1914 as such an important year?

As recorded at Luke 21:24, Jesus said: "Jerusalem will be trampled on by the nations, until the appointed times of

*What Does the Bible Really Teach?*

the nations ["the times of the Gentiles," *King James Version*] are fulfilled." Jerusalem had been the capital city of the Jewish nation—the seat of rulership of the line of kings from the house of King David. (Psalm 48:1, 2) However, these kings were unique among national leaders. They sat on "Jehovah's throne" as representatives of God himself. (1 Chronicles 29:23) Jerusalem was thus a symbol of Jehovah's rulership.

How and when, though, did God's rulership begin to be "trampled on by the nations"? This happened in 607 B.C.E. when Jerusalem was conquered by the Babylonians. "Jehovah's throne" became vacant, and the line of kings who descended from David was interrupted. (2 Kings 25:1-26)

## "SEVEN TIMES"

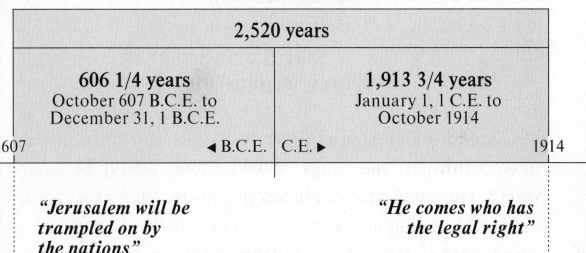

| 2,520 years | |
|---|---|
| **606 1/4 years** <br> October 607 B.C.E. to <br> December 31, 1 B.C.E. | **1,913 3/4 years** <br> January 1, 1 C.E. to <br> October 1914 |

607 ◄ B.C.E. │ C.E. ► 1914

*"Jerusalem will be trampled on by the nations"*

*"He comes who has the legal right"*

Would this 'trampling' go on forever? No, for the prophecy of Ezekiel said regarding Jerusalem's last king, Zedekiah: "Remove the turban, and lift off the crown. . . . It will certainly become no one's until he comes who has the legal right, and I must give it to him." (Ezekiel 21:26, 27) The one who has "the legal right" to the Davidic crown is Christ Jesus. (Luke 1:32, 33) So the 'trampling' would end when Jesus became King.

When would that grand event occur? Jesus showed that the Gentiles would rule for a fixed period of time. The account in Daniel chapter 4 holds the key to knowing how long that period would last. It relates a prophetic dream experienced by King Nebuchadnezzar of Babylon. He saw an immense tree that was chopped down. Its stump could not grow because it was banded with iron and copper. An angel declared: "Let *seven times* pass over it."—Daniel 4: 10-16.

In the Bible, trees are sometimes used to represent rulership. (Ezekiel 17:22-24; 31:2-5) So the chopping down of the symbolic tree represents how God's rulership, as expressed through the kings at Jerusalem, would be interrupted. However, the vision served notice that this 'trampling of Jerusalem' would be temporary—a period of "seven times." How long a period is that?

Revelation 12:6, 14 indicates that three and a half times

*What Does the Bible Really Teach?*

equal "a thousand two hundred and sixty days." "Seven times" would therefore last twice as long, or 2,520 days. But the Gentile nations did not stop 'trampling' on God's rulership a mere 2,520 days after Jerusalem's fall. Evidently, then, this prophecy covers a much longer period of time. On the basis of Numbers 14:34 and Ezekiel 4:6, which speak of "a day for a year," the "seven times" would cover 2,520 *years*.

The 2,520 years began in October 607 B.C.E., when Jerusalem fell to the Babylonians and the Davidic king was taken off his throne. The period ended in October 1914. At that time, "the appointed times of the nations" ended, and Jesus Christ was installed as God's heavenly King.* —Psalm 2:1-6; Daniel 7:13, 14.

Just as Jesus predicted, his "presence" as heavenly King has been marked by dramatic world developments—war, famine, earthquakes, pestilences. (Matthew 24:3-8; Luke 21:11) Such developments bear powerful testimony to the fact that 1914 indeed marked the birth of God's heavenly Kingdom and the beginning of "the last days" of this present wicked system of things.—2 Timothy 3:1-5.

---

* From October 607 B.C.E. to October 1 B.C.E. is 606 years. Since there is no zero year, from October 1 B.C.E. to October 1914 C.E. is 1,914 years. By adding 606 years and 1,914 years, we get 2,520 years. For information on Jerusalem's fall in 607 B.C.E., see the article "Chronology" in *Insight on the Scriptures,* published by Jehovah's Witnesses.

# Who Is Michael the Archangel?

THE spirit creature called Michael is not mentioned often in the Bible. However, when he is referred to, he is in action. In the book of Daniel, Michael is battling wicked angels; in the letter of Jude, he is disputing with Satan; and in Revelation, he is waging war with the Devil and his demons. By defending Jehovah's rulership and fighting God's enemies, Michael lives up to the meaning of his name —"Who Is Like God?" But who is Michael?

At times, individuals are known by more than one name. For example, the patriarch Jacob is also known as Israel, and the apostle Peter, as Simon. (Genesis 49:1, 2; Matthew 10:2) Likewise, the Bible indicates that Michael is another name for Jesus Christ, before and after his life on earth. Let us consider Scriptural reasons for drawing that conclusion.

*Archangel.* God's Word refers to Michael "the archangel." (Jude 9) This term means "chief angel." Notice that Michael is called *the* archangel. This suggests that there is only one such angel. In fact, the term "archangel" occurs in the Bible only in the singular, never in the plural. Moreover, Jesus is linked with the office of archangel. Regarding the resurrected Lord Jesus Christ, 1 Thessalonians 4:16 states: "The Lord himself will descend from heaven

*What Does the Bible Really Teach?*

with a commanding call, with an archangel's voice." Thus the voice of Jesus is described as being that of an archangel. This scripture therefore suggests that Jesus himself is the archangel Michael.

*Army Leader.* The Bible states that "Michael and *his* angels battled with the dragon . . . and its angels." (Revelation 12:7) Thus, Michael is the Leader of an army of faithful angels. Revelation also describes Jesus as the Leader of an army of faithful angels. (Revelation 19:14-16) And the apostle Paul specifically mentions "the Lord Jesus" and "his powerful angels." (2 Thessalonians 1:7; Matthew 16: 27; 24:31; 1 Peter 3:22) So the Bible speaks of both Michael and "his angels" and Jesus and "his angels." (Matthew 13: 41) Since God's Word nowhere indicates that there are two armies of faithful angels in heaven—one headed by Michael and one headed by Jesus—it is logical to conclude that Michael is none other than Jesus Christ in his heavenly role.*

---

* More information showing that the name Michael applies to God's Son is found in Volume 2, pages 393-4, of *Insight on the Scriptures,* published by Jehovah's Witnesses.

# Identifying "Babylon the Great"

THE book of Revelation contains expressions that are not to be understood literally. (Revelation 1:1) For example, it mentions a woman with the name "Babylon the Great" written on her forehead. This woman is said to be sitting on "crowds and nations." (Revelation 17:1, 5, 15) Since no literal woman could do this, Babylon the Great must be symbolic. So, what does this symbolic harlot represent?

At Revelation 17:18, the same figurative woman is described as "the great city that has a kingdom over the kings of the earth." The term "city" indicates an organized group of people. Since this "great city" has control over "the kings of the earth," the woman named Babylon the Great must be an influential organization that is international in scope. It can rightly be called a world empire. What kind of empire? A religious one. Notice how some related passages in the book of Revelation lead us to this conclusion.

An empire can be political, commercial, or religious. The woman named Babylon the Great is not a political empire because God's Word states that "the kings of the earth," or the political elements of this world, "committed fornication" with her. Her fornication refers to the alliances she has made with the rulers of this earth and explains why she is called "the great harlot."—Revelation 17: 1, 2; James 4:4.

Babylon the Great cannot be a commercial empire because the "merchants of the earth," representing the commercial elements, will be mourning her at the time of her

*What Does the Bible Really Teach?*

destruction. In fact, both kings and merchants are described as looking at Babylon the Great from "a distance." (Revelation 18:3, 9, 10, 15-17) Therefore, it is reasonable to conclude that Babylon the Great is, not a political or a commercial empire, but a religious one.

The religious identity of Babylon the Great is further confirmed by the statement that she misleads all the nations by means of her "spiritistic practice." (Revelation 18:23) Since all forms of spiritism are demon-inspired, it is not surprising that the Bible calls Babylon the Great "a dwelling place of demons." (Revelation 18:2; Deuteronomy 18:10-12) This empire is also described as being actively opposed to true religion, persecuting "prophets" and "holy ones." (Revelation 18:24) In fact, Babylon the Great has such deep hatred for true religion that she violently persecutes and even murders "the witnesses of Jesus." (Revelation 17:6) Hence, this woman named Babylon the Great clearly represents the world empire of false religion, which includes all religions that stand in opposition to Jehovah God.

## Was Jesus Born in December?

THE Bible does not tell us when Jesus was born. However, it does give us sound reason to conclude that his birth did not take place in December.

Consider the weather conditions at that time of the year in Bethlehem, where Jesus was born. The Jewish month of Chislev (corresponding to November/December) was a month with cold and rainy weather. The month after that was Tebeth (December/January). It saw the lowest temperatures of the year, with occasional snows in the highlands. Let us see what the Bible tells us about the climate of that region.

The Bible writer Ezra shows that Chislev was indeed a month known for cold and rainy weather. After stating that a crowd had gathered in Jerusalem "in the ninth month [Chislev] on the twentieth day of the month," Ezra reports that people were "shivering . . . on account of the showers of rain." Concerning weather conditions at that time of the year, the congregated people themselves said: "It is the season of showers of rain, and it is not possible to stand outside." (Ezra 10:9, 13; Jeremiah 36:22) No wonder shepherds living in that part of the world made sure that they and their flocks were no longer out of doors at night when December came around!

The Bible reports, however, that shepherds were in the fields tending their flocks on the night of Jesus' birth. In fact, the Bible writer Luke shows that at that time, shepherds were "living out of doors and keeping watches in the night over their flocks" near Bethlehem. (Luke 2:8-12) No-

*What Does the Bible Really Teach?*

tice that the shepherds were actually *living* out of doors, not just strolling outside during the day. They had their flocks in the fields *at night*. Does that description of outdoor living fit the chilly and rainy weather conditions of Bethlehem in December? No, it does not. So the circumstances surrounding Jesus' birth indicate that he was not born in December.*

God's Word tells us precisely when Jesus died, but it gives little direct indication as to when he was born. This brings to mind King Solomon's words: "A name is better than good oil, and the day of death than the day of one's being born." (Ecclesiastes 7:1) It is not surprising, then, that the Bible provides many details about Jesus' ministry and death but few details about the time of his birth.

---

* For more information, see pages 176-9 of *Reasoning From the Scriptures,* published by Jehovah's Witnesses.

## Should We Celebrate Holidays?

THE Bible is not the source of popular religious and secular holidays that are celebrated in many parts of the world today. What, then, is the origin of such celebrations? If you have access to a library, you will find it interesting to note what reference books say about holidays that are popular where you live. Consider a few examples.

***Easter.*** "There is no indication of the observance of the Easter festival in the New Testament," states *The Encyclopædia Britannica*. How did Easter get started? It is rooted in pagan worship. While this holiday is supposed to commemorate Jesus' resurrection, the customs associated with the Easter season are not Christian. For instance, concerning the popular "Easter bunny," *The Catholic Encyclopedia* says: "The rabbit is a pagan symbol and has always been an emblem of fertility."

***New Year's Celebrations.*** The date and customs associated with New Year's celebrations vary from one country to another. Regarding the origin of this celebration, *The World Book Encyclopedia* states: "The Roman ruler Julius Caesar established January 1 as New Year's Day in 46 B.C. The Romans dedicated this day to Janus, the god of gates, doors, and beginnings. The month of January was named after Janus, who had two faces—one looking forward and the other looking backward." So New Year's celebrations are founded on pagan traditions.

***Halloween.*** *The Encyclopedia Americana* says: "Elements of the customs connected with Halloween can be traced to a Druid [ancient Celtic priesthood] ceremony in pre-Christian times. The Celts had festivals for two major gods —a sun god and a god of the dead . . . , whose festival was held on November 1, the beginning of the Celtic New Year.

*What Does the Bible Really Teach?*

The festival of the dead was gradually incorporated into Christian ritual."

***Other Holidays.*** It is not possible to discuss all the observances held throughout the world. However, holidays that exalt humans or human organizations are not acceptable to Jehovah. (Jeremiah 17:5-7; Acts 10:25, 26) Keep in mind, too, that the origin of religious celebrations has a bearing on whether they please God or not. (Isaiah 52:11; Revelation 18:4) The Bible principles mentioned in Chapter 16 of this book will help you to determine how God views participation in holidays of a secular nature.

# Would you welcome more information?

## Write Jehovah's Witnesses at the appropriate address below.

**ALASKA 99507:** 2552 East 48th Ave., Anchorage.
**ALBANIA:** Kutia postare 118, Tiranë.
**ANGOLA:** Caixa Postal 6877, Luanda Sul.
**ANTIGUA:** Box 119, St. Johns.
**ARGENTINA:** Casilla de Correo 83 (Suc. 27B), 1427 Buenos Aires.
**AUSTRALIA:** Box 280, Ingleburn, NSW 1890.
**AUSTRIA:** Postfach 67, A-1134 Vienna.
**BAHAMAS:** Box N-1247, Nassau, N.P.
**BARBADOS, W.I.:** Crusher Site Road, Prospect, St. James.
**BELGIUM:** rue d'Argile-Potaardestraat 60, B-1950 Kraainem.
**BENIN, REP. OF:** 06 B.P. 1131, Akpakpa pk3, Cotonou.
**BOLIVIA:** Casilla 6397, Santa Cruz.
**BRAZIL:** Caixa Postal 92, 18270-970 Tatuí, SP.
**BRITAIN:** The Ridgeway, London NW7 1RN.
**CAMEROON:** B.P. 889, Douala.
**CANADA:** Box 4100, Halton Hills (Georgetown), Ontario L7G 4Y4.
**CENTRAL AFRICAN REPUBLIC:** B.P. 662, Bangui.
**CHILE:** Casilla 267, Puente Alto.
**COLOMBIA:** Apartado Postal 85058, Bogotá 8, D.C.
**CONGO, DEMOCRATIC REPUBLIC OF:** B.P. 634, Limete, Kinshasa.
**COSTA RICA:** Apartado 187-3006, Barreal, Heredia.
**CÔTE D'IVOIRE (IVORY COAST), WEST AFRICA:** 06 B P 393, Abidjan 06.
**CROATIA:** p.p. 58, HR-10090 Zagreb-Susedgrad.
**CURAÇAO, NETHERLANDS ANTILLES:** P.O. Box 4708, Willemstad.
**CYPRUS:** P.O. Box 11033, CY-2550 Dali.
**CZECH REPUBLIC:** P.O. Box 90, 198 21 Prague 9.
**DENMARK:** Stenhusvej 28, DK-4300 Holbæk.
**DOMINICAN REPUBLIC:** Apartado 1742, Santo Domingo.
**ECUADOR:** Casilla 09-01-1334, Guayaquil.
**EL SALVADOR:** Apartado Postal 401, San Salvador.
**ESTONIA:** Postbox 1075, 10302 Tallinn.
**ETHIOPIA:** P.O. Box 5522, Addis Ababa.
**FIJI:** Box 23, Suva.
**FINLAND:** Postbox 68, FIN-01301 Vantaa.
**FRANCE:** B.P. 625, F-27406 Louviers cedex.
**GERMANY:** Niederselters, Am Steinfels, D-65618 Selters.
**GHANA:** P. O. Box GP 760, Accra.
**GREECE:** 77 Kifisias Ave., GR-151 24, Marousi, Athens.
**GUADELOUPE:** Monmain, 97180 Sainte Anne.
**GUAM 96913:** 143 Jehovah St., Barrigada.
**GUATEMALA:** Apartado postal 711, 01901 Guatemala.
**GUYANA:** 352-360 Tyrell St., Republic Park Phase 2 EBD.
**GUYANE FRANÇAISE (FRENCH GUIANA):** 328 CD2, Route du Tigre, 97300 Cayenne.
**HAITI:** Post Box 185, Port-au-Prince.
**HAWAII 96819:** 2055 Kam IV Rd., Honolulu.
**HONDURAS:** Apartado 147, Tegucigalpa.
**HONG KONG:** 4 Kent Road, Kowloon Tong.
**HUNGARY:** H-1631 Budapest, Pf. 20.
**INDIA:** Post Box 6440, Yelahanka, Bangalore 560 064, KAR.
**INDONESIA:** P.O. Box 2105, Jakarta 10001.
**IRELAND:** Newcastle, Greystones, Co. Wicklow.
**ISRAEL:** P.O. Box 29345, Tel Aviv 61293.
**ITALY:** Via della Bufalotta 1281, I-00138 Rome RM.
**JAMAICA:** P. O. Box 103, Old Harbour, St. Catherine.

**JAPAN:** 1271 Nakashinden, Ebina City, Kanagawa Pref., 243-0496.
**KENYA:** P. O. Box 47788, GPO Nairobi 00100.
**KOREA, REPUBLIC OF:** Box 33 Pyungtaek P. O., Kyunggido, 450-600.
**LIBERIA:** P. O. Box 10-0380, 1000 Monrovia 10.
**LUXEMBOURG:** B. P. 2186, L-1021 Luxembourg, G. D.
**MADAGASCAR:** B.P. 116, 105 Ivato.
**MALAWI:** Box 30749, Lilongwe 3.
**MALAYSIA:** Peti Surat No. 580, 75760 Melaka.
**MARTINIQUE:** 20, rue de la Cour Campêche, 97200 Fort de France.
**MAURITIUS:** Rue Baissac, Petit Verger, Pointe aux Sables.
**MEXICO:** Apartado Postal 896, 06002 Mexico, D. F.
**MOZAMBIQUE:** Caixa Postal 2600, Maputo.
**MYANMAR:** P.O. Box 62, Yangon.
**NETHERLANDS:** Noordbargerstraat 77, NL-7812 AA Emmen.
**NEW CALEDONIA:** BP 1741, 98874 Mont Dore.
**NEW ZEALAND:** P O Box 75-142, Manurewa.
**NICARAGUA:** Apartado 3587, Managua.
**NIGERIA:** P.M.B. 1090, Benin City 300001, Edo State.
**NORWAY:** Gaupeveien 24, N-1914 Ytre Enebakk.
**PANAMA:** Apartado 6-2671, Zona 6A, El Dorado.
**PAPUA NEW GUINEA:** P. O. Box 636, Boroko, NCD 111.
**PARAGUAY:** Casilla de Correo 482, 1209 Asunción.
**PERU:** Apartado 18-1055, Lima 18.
**PHILIPPINES, REPUBLIC OF:** P. O. Box 2044, 1060 Manila.
**POLAND:** ul. Warszawska 14, PL-05-830 Nadarzyn.
**PORTUGAL:** Apartado 91, P-2766-955 Estoril.
**PUERTO RICO 00970:** P.O. Box 3980, Guaynabo.
**ROMANIA:** Căsuţa Poştală nr. 132, Oficiul Poştal nr. 39, Bucureşti.
**RUSSIA:** ul. Srednyaya 6, p. Solnechnoye, 197739 St. Petersburg.
**RWANDA:** B.P. 529, Kigali.
**SLOVAKIA:** P. O. Box 2, 830 04 Bratislava 34.
**SLOVENIA:** Poljanska cesta 77 A, p.p. 2019, SI-1001 Ljubljana.
**SOLOMON ISLANDS:** P.O. Box 166, Honiara.
**SOUTH AFRICA:** Private Bag X2067, Krugersdorp, 1740.
**SPAIN:** Apartado 132, 28850 Torrejón de Ardoz (Madrid).
**SRI LANKA, REP. OF:** 711 Station Road, Wattala 11300.
**SURINAME:** P.O. Box 2914, Paramaribo.
**SWEDEN:** Box 5, SE-732 21 Arboga.
**SWITZERLAND:** P.O. Box 225, CH-3602 Thun.
**TAHITI:** B.P. 7715, 98719 Taravao.
**TAIWAN 327:** 3-12, Lin 7, Shetze Village, Hsinwu.
**TANZANIA:** Box 7992, Dar es Salaam.
**THAILAND:** 69/1 Soi Phasuk, Sukhumwit Rd., Soi 2, Bangkok 10110.
**TOGO, WEST AFRICA:** B.P. 2983, Lomé.
**TRINIDAD AND TOBAGO, REP. OF:** Lower Rapsey Street & Laxmi Lane, Curepe.
**UKRAINE:** P.O. Box 246, 79000 Lviv.
**UNITED STATES OF AMERICA:** 25 Columbia Heights, Brooklyn, NY 11201-2483.
**URUGUAY:** Casilla 17030, 12500 Montevideo.
**VENEZUELA:** Apartado 20.364, Caracas, DC 1020A.
**ZAMBIA:** Box 33459, Lusaka 10101.
**ZIMBABWE:** Private Bag WG-5001, Westgate.